Praise for
Happily Ever After

"As a two-time cancer survivor and cofounder of the charity organization Grassroot Soccer, I know the undeniable value of gratitude. Whether you are giving or receiving, *Happily Ever After* shows us what I have come to accept as truth—in order to fully live a happy life, you must acknowledge the gifts that life has to offer and be thankful for all of them . . . big and small."

—ETHAN ZOHN, 2002 winner of *Survivor: Africa*

"This book is a wonderful reminder that in everything we do we should give thanks. From the beautiful life-changers to the everyday little things to the struggles that break us down, EVERYTHING is a gift and it's important for us to acknowledge that."

—ALI LANDRY, mom, actress, and Miss USA 1996

"*Happily Ever After* is profound, passionate, and practical. These stories of gratitude will move, inspire, and touch you—you will not be able to live your life the same way."

—LEE M. BROWER, Founder, Empowered Wealth, LC, Business Family Coach, author, speaker, and featured teacher on gratitude in the book and movie *The Secret*

"Trista is someone who exudes light and joy, and I'm grateful that she's harnessed some of that for this uplifting, full-of-healthy-tidbits book about the importance and fun of having an optimistic view of the world. Thanks, Trista!"

—KIMBERLY WILLIAMS-PAISLEY, actress, director, writer, and mom

HAPPILY
EVER AFTER

HAPPILY
EVER AFTER

*The Life-Changing Power
of a Grateful Heart*

TRISTA SUTTER

Da Capo
∞
LIFE
LONG

A MEMBER OF THE PERSEUS BOOKS GROUP

Designed by Linda Mark
Set in 11.5 point ITC Usherwood Std by the Perseus Books Group

Library of Congress Cataloging-in-Publication Data
Sutter, Trista.
 Happily ever after : the life-changing power of a grateful heart / Trista Sutter.
 pages cm
 ISBN 978-0-7382-1665-2 (hardback)—ISBN 978-0-7382-1666-9 (e-book)
1. Gratitude. 2. Happiness. 3. Women—Psychology. I. Title.
 BF575.G68S98 2013
 179'.9—dc23

2013025477

First Da Capo Press edition 2013

Published by Da Capo Press
A Member of the Perseus Books Group
www.dacapopress.com

Da Capo Press books are available at special discounts for bulk purchases in the US by corporations, institutions, and other organizations. For more information, please contact the Special Markets Department at the Perseus Books Group, 2300 Chestnut Street, Suite 200, Philadelphia, PA 19103, or call (800) 810-4145, ext. 5000, or e-mail special.markets@perseusbooks.com.

10 9 8 7 6 5 4 3 2 1

*Happiness is the spiritual experience
of living every minute with love, grace, and gratitude.*

—DENIS WAITLEY

Contents

Contents

Thank-You Notes
Are Better Than Roses

God gave you a gift of 86,400 seconds today.

Have you used one to say thank you?

——WILLIAM A. WARD

BEFORE APPEARING ON *THE BACHELOR* I WAS A SINGLE girl living in the exciting world of South Florida. I had great friends, a supportive family, and two demanding jobs: I spent my days working as a pediatric physical therapist at Miami Children's Hospital, and my nights rehearsing or performing as a Miami Heat dancer.

My schedule was full, and I was doing what I thought I loved, but I felt empty and bored. Then one night fate spoke to me through my television. I was watching the entertainment-news show *Extra,* trying to unwind after a long day at the hospital, when a Hollywood casting director came on to talk about a new reality show. I had been a fan of *The Real World*, but this new show wasn't just a social experiment recorded for the world to see. It was about one guy getting to know twenty-five girls in the hope of finding a fiancée. That's right . . . one guy, twenty-five girls. Obviously a little crazy, but when the casting director mentioned international travel and luxurious living quarters, I figured it would surely beat my lonely apartment.

As hockey great Wayne Gretzky once said, "You miss 100 percent of the shots you don't take," so I headed straight to my computer to type in the link that had flashed on the screen.

What was the worst that could happen? If they rejected my application, I would just continue living in my unhappy rut, hoping to find a way out.

For a few weeks, I did just that. But then the casting people called asking for a video, photos, and eventually a face-to-face meeting. After a slew of interviews and tests, including blood work and incredibly long psychological exams, I got the news that they were actually interested in little ol' me joining their upcoming adventure. They liked me. They really liked me. (Sorry—I've always loved Sally Field.) Now all that was left to do was ask for a leave of absence from the hospital (which was thoughtfully granted) and make sure I had everything I needed for a couple months away.

Going into it, I had no intention of falling in love with a stranger I would know for only six weeks and whom I would be sharing with twenty-four other ladies, but as the days passed, my mind-set changed. I got to know more and more about Alex Michel, and I liked what I learned. In real life, I would've done as I usually did: take it slow. But in this situation, there wasn't a job to report to or basketball games to perform at, gossip sessions on the phone with my girlfriends, visits to the gym, or even couch time in front of the TV to take up my downtime. This relationship was my focus, and I actually quite enjoyed it.

In early 2002, I found myself visiting "fantasy suites," taking helicopter rides, traveling to exotic destinations, and enjoying the glamorous world of professional hair and makeup. Alex was a good conversationalist, highly educated, nice-looking, and well traveled: all things I was looking for in a partner. It seemed as though we had similar values and goals, and I grew increasingly intrigued.

Two days before we were to tape the ending of the show, we had our last date. There was still one other girl left, and their time together was scheduled for the next evening. I wanted to know where I stood in comparison to her, so I asked him. Point-blank.

He told me that if he had to make a choice at that very moment, he would choose me. (Duh—what else was he going to say?)

I left that night with the utmost confidence that his feelings wouldn't change, no matter what happened on his date with the other remaining woman.

Two nights later, I walked down the pathway to the final rose ceremony. True, I had known this guy for only six weeks, but we had developed a real connection and I was fully prepared to get engaged. It wasn't a joke to me. It wasn't a way to launch my acting career or a new business. It was my life.

Standing across from Alex, I listened intently to the words that came out of his mouth. He started out by telling me how much he enjoyed our time together. Then there was a pause. I thought it was a lead-up to a proposal, but boy, was I ever wrong! Instead, he told me that our story was coming to an end, and that he was sorry.

Dagger to the heart, and on national television! I was destroyed. The crew filmed me and my tears in what would become a classic *Bachelor* scene: the runner-up crying her eyes out in the back of the exiting limo, signifying the end to their reality show journey.

"I'm okay," I said. "I'm just sad."

I soon realized that I didn't believe my own words.

Back in my hotel room, I wallowed in my sadness. Everything had been taken away from me—or so I thought. I had no idea that the universe was setting me up for what would be the most incredible, enriching experience of my life. What I thought was a loss was a total gain, but I couldn't see anything through the tears.

In real life, you get to say good-bye. On the show, you aren't stopped from doing so, but once your fate is announced, you are whooshed away before you've had a chance to process what has just happened. Six weeks of your life and—poof—it's over.

I had gone to LA for an adventure and ended up with a broken heart. It wasn't fun, but it was wonderfully motivating. I knew more than ever before what kind of person I was looking for and what kind of person I had become. I had enjoyed the glitz of my new existence but, deep down, I yearned for something much simpler but so much harder to find: my own happy family.

For the next three months, the footage was edited and a series was created. Contractually bound by confidentiality, I had to keep my friends and family in the dark and return to life as I knew it before I met Alex Michel. It's amazing how much happier life can be when you gain some perspective.

As my past life played out on national television, I watched every week with my friends and family and found myself gradually getting over the heartache. On the night of the finale, I tuned in along with a gaggle of my friends, at a special viewing party. That night my cell phone rang. It was Mike Fleiss, the executive producer. He wanted to know if I would be interested in the chance to turn the tables and become the first Bachelorette.

I didn't hesitate. "Seriously?! Sign me up!"

With the ABC television network at the helm of my search for love, I knew I would be drastically improving my odds. After all, people were being paid to scour the country to find guys who fit my "type." I didn't have that kind of time and, buried in student loans, I certainly didn't have that kind of money.

So I asked for another leave of absence and when that was politely refused, I said good-bye to the PT department at Miami Children's Hospital and set sail for the West Coast . . . a spot I had always dreamed of calling home.

While I worked out the legalities with the production company's powers that be, I hit the gym, met new friends, and waited for the day I would stand in front of my mansion-away-from-home, hearing host Chris Harrison say, "Let the journey begin." October 10, 2002, was that day.

In a long, black Carmen Marc Valvo dress and a more than ten-carat diamond necklace bigger than my earlobe, I was introduced to twenty-five charming bachelors. One of them was a stunner who was so thoroughly outside of his comfort zone that he forgot to tell me his name. But after I heard it for the first time, I would never forget it: Ryan Sutter. He stepped out of the limo and told me I looked "ravishing." I couldn't remember a time that I had even heard that word in a sentence, but it sounded so romantic and genuine, and I bought it—hook, line, and sinker. His crystal-blue eyes, firefighter résumé, NFL muscles, and the poem he handed me during our first solo chat didn't hurt his cause either. For the next six weeks, he continued to stand out among the crowd, a crowd of eligible men who had left their homes and jobs to test the relationship waters with me.

With cameras following our every move, I got to know as much as I could about each of the men who had signed up to join me on this crazy ride. Ryan had been a front-runner since the first night, but after holding that position myself for much of the journey I shared with Alex Michel and then getting the rug pulled out from underneath me, I decided to keep my heart as open as I possibly could and not make a final decision until the very end.

I fully immersed myself in the search for love. I hoped to find someone who made me laugh and had a strong family bond. Someone who wanted to create babies out of our love and show the world what it meant to be a good father. Someone who made me feel special and safe and full of fluttering butterflies. Someone who was kind, honorable, trustworthy, and athletic. Someone I couldn't stop thinking about no matter whom I was with or what I was doing or where I was in my travels.

After narrowing down the playing field week after week, I couldn't deny the inevitable. I had told myself before I started that I wanted to walk off into the sunset with a man I couldn't live without. At the end of the six weeks, I got all that and more.

On the night of the final rose ceremony, I said good-bye to Charlie, the only other man remaining, and waited patiently for Ryan to arrive. I was on a platform surrounded by candles and flowers, but all I could think about was the gorgeousness of the man I had completely and utterly fallen for. I will never forget the intensity of the smile that took over my face when Ryan started walking down the stairs toward me. It was happiness in its purest form, and not only because he brought me such joy, but because I could finally reveal the depth of my love to the man who had captured my heart.

I had worked very hard to keep my feelings to myself, constantly worrying that if I shared them with Ryan they might change, just as Alex's had for me on the final day taping *The Bachelor* nine months earlier. I had wanted to protect Ryan from that kind of pain, but soon found out that I had been unintentionally torturing him in another way: through ambiguity.

From about the fourth week of the process, he continually confessed his developing love for me. I tried to show him through my actions that I felt the same, but he needed more and I didn't know how much until it was almost too late. Thank goodness I didn't know at the time, but the day I was to reveal my final decision, Ryan disappeared. He had hit a wall of frustration and decided to quiet his mind away from prying producers and the chaos of the show. He made his way to a neighboring hotel and tried to get some clarity poolside. As someone who has been in those very shoes, I don't blame him for one millisecond. The good news is that he showed up when it mattered most—when I could finally tell him that I had fallen for him.

During the rose ceremony, I asked to hold his hands and took a big, deep breath before saying what I'd been keeping hidden in my heart:

Ryan, this day is a day I have dreamt about my entire life. Since I was a little girl, I've had visions of a man who I could see my future with, but someone whose face was always blurred. Until now. Now, I not only see his face, but I see a future of dreams come true. I see smiles and laughter. I see babies and grandbabies. I see comfort and safety. I see a white dress and I see it with you.

He interrupted, "You do?" with a big smile on his face. Then he let me finish pouring out my thoughts.

You've stepped out of my dreams and into my world, and I want to thank you for standing by my side when I couldn't give you any verbal reciprocation of your feelings. But my walls have finally crumbled and I can now tell you without reservation that I'm in love with you. I hope with all my heart that you feel the same and that you want to spend the rest of your life with me, as I do with you.

I can't help but giggle when I replay that moment in my mind, because he was *so* ready for me to stop talking. (Things haven't changed much.)

After asking if I was done and giving me one of the kisses that had made me fall in love with him, he said:

I started down this road hoping for love, and I think I was only able to make it to the end because I found it. You were my strength. You were my inspiration. You were the breath of my voice and there's a place in my heart, a space now that only you can fill. Trista, I love you with every ounce of who I am and offer you my hand and my heart and soul and my love forever, if you'll have it.

So, Trista Nicole Rehn, will you marry me?

I can't remember how many times I said yes (although I know it's on a dusty VHS tape somewhere out there), but I did . . . over and over again. My fairy tale, or at least its beginning, had finally come true.

We were engaged on November 11, 2002, and after a grueling three months apart (to conceal our happy ending from the public and the media), we were ecstatic to start our life together—a life of true reality, not one that included an entourage of cameramen and producers.

I've been around for more than forty years and I am certain that happily ever after isn't always glamorous. It has nothing to do with whether you can afford or fit into a dress right off the runway. It isn't based on how many times you've had your hair and makeup done, what you get paid (or not) to do with your time, how many square feet your house is, or the number of invitations you've had to talk to Larry King, Diane Sawyer, Barbara Walters, or Ellen DeGeneres.

Away from the cameras, away from the spotlight . . . everything was different. I can't tell you what happened to Cinderella and her prince after their fairy-tale ending, but in the case of Ryan and me, happily ever after was about building a home and a family and a peaceful life together. Our off-camera lifestyle now includes a daily balancing act of work and play, a house in need of constant tidying, bills to pay, mail to open, kids needing Mommy and Daddy, a dog who could probably use a bath and some belly rubs, and a marriage that needs just as much attention, if not more, than everything else on my long list of things to do.

Do I enjoy bits of pampering as an annual tradition on my birthday, treat myself to manicures so that my temptation to nibble at my nails is curbed, and take advantage of date nights when we can get a sitter? Heck, yes! But my days are not full of long, luxurious bubble baths, hours relaxing with a bowl of popcorn and the latest chick flick in a glamorous home theater, dinner parties catered by my personal chef, shopping sprees, or even massages.

Above all else, I'm proud to be a mom, wife, daughter, and friend. Maybe if I won the lottery, I could focus on those roles alone, but since that has yet to happen, I'm also required, as so many of us are, to take on the additional roles of housekeeper, travel agent, psychologist, spokesperson, peacemaker, chauffeur, accountant, secretary, teacher, chef, manager, nurse, designer, and cheerleader.

And while I may have found my prince and landed at the center of some extraordinary moments, I have also suffered and struggled through my fair share of disappointment and pain.

The universe has taught me so much, and undoubtedly will continue to do so. The main thing I've learned about what makes for a happy life, right up there with good health and lots of love, is gratitude.

My intent here is to share not only the lessons I've learned, but also those of my friends and family, those of strangers, and even some of the teachings of some of the world's most enlightened authors, philosophers, poets, and educators. I will never claim to be an expert, but you won't have to take it from only me; there is plenty of research out there to back up the benefits of a grateful heart.

I just hope that after reading these pages you will walk away with a positive outlook on life and all it has to offer. Then, if you've taken anything I've said to heart, you will lay your head down at night feeling the same way I do: like the luckiest person on the block, thankful for all the little blessings that make up your world.

A Conscious Choice

I am not what happened to me.
I am what I choose to become.

—CARL GUSTAV JUNG

CHAPTER ONE

EVERY MORNING, I WAKE UP AND WONDER WHAT THE day will bring. Every night, whether I've had one of those days, a day I would love to completely forget, or a day that made my cheeks hurt from smiling, I make it a point to remember my favorite part of the day. I've been posting these thoughts, my own personal expressions of gratitude, almost every night on Twitter and Facebook under the hashtag #favepartofday for the past four years. It may sound silly, but it's my way of focusing on the positive. As Olympian Jesse Owens once said, "Find the good. It's all around you. Find it, showcase it, and you'll start believing it."

My days aren't always perfect, but I believe wholeheartedly in what Jesse said. By actively noting my favorite part of each day, I make myself more receptive to the joys of life—from the second I wake up until just before I send out my nightly post. This simple act makes me accountable to searching for and sharing shining moments, and helps me realize through a changed perspective that I have so much to be grateful for.

On May 10, 2009, that was certainly the case. It was about a month after I had welcomed a beautiful baby girl, my second child, into the world, and it was a day of celebration.

Blakesley Grace Sutter was celebrating five weeks of life, and I was celebrating Mother's Day for the first time as the proud mom of two. It was a day I had dreamed about for most of my life, and I cherished it that much more because the path to reach it hadn't always been an easy one to follow. Looking back, though, I see that all the pieces found their place in my life at just the right times—each piece adding more and more meaning along the way.

Finding someone to walk hand-in-hand with down the path was the piece that eluded me the longest (thirty years), but thanks to a network-television matchmaker, producers who saw something in me, and an open mind, I found Ryan. Crazy? Definitely. Worth it? You bet!

After saying "I do" and taking a couple years to enjoy our newlywed status, Ryan and I were ready to add the next piece of the puzzle to our lives: parenthood. Like the children's playground song says, "First comes love, then comes marriage, then comes baby in a baby carriage," we believed that nature would automatically take over after we were married and we could throw caution to the wind. No birth control = new baby, right? Yeah . . . not so much.

But we were determined to start a family and actively pursued our goal.

Did sex become a chore? Yes. Even with a husband as good-looking as I think mine is, when sex is a requirement, it becomes more like a duty and less like the stuff you see in the movies.

Did frustration rear its ugly head? Yes.

Did we undergo painful and embarrassing blood tests, semen tests (Ryan), acupuncture, and intrauterine inseminations (me)? Yes, yes, yes, and yes.

We did everything we could until we couldn't do anything new. We finally came to grips with the fact that we needed help, so we sought out Drs. William Schoolcraft and Eric Surrey at the Colorado Center for Reproductive Medicine. They have one of the most successful fertility clinics in the country and, luckily, they are practically our neighbors. (Okay, it takes two hours to get to their office from our house, but when you live in the mountains, two hours is practically your backyard.)

Before we could start the process, there were more tests and a particularly excruciating procedure involving one of the things I truly hate: needles. The good news: After the procedure, our options (aka my cervix) literally opened up. Ryan's guys were able to reach their destination and get the job done. We were pregnant!

I couldn't have been happier, but my body didn't feel the same way.

For the first sixteen weeks of my pregnant life, I was on the couch, feeling much the way I had back in college after a night like my twenty-first birthday, when I lost my sanity and attempted twenty-one shots (I made it to nineteen, and yes, I know, I was an idiot). Every second of every day was an ongoing battle with nausea that wouldn't disappear, no matter what I tried—and I tried it all. I ate raw ginger and Preggie Pops, Popsicles, and boxes of Froot Loops—sometimes all in one sitting. I was also reminded to drink what felt like gallons of water each day, but I've always struggled with downing glasses of water, especially when my stomach is queasy. To make matters worse, I didn't brush my teeth or change out of my pajamas for what seemed like months (official apologies to both my husband and my dentist, Dr. Haerter). I felt like life was draining out of me rather than growing inside of me.

Thankfully, the torment of an unsettled stomach finally resolved. For a few months, I was able to put a smile on my face, get out of the house, and quit complaining.

But wait: after an oral glucose test at twenty-nine weeks, I was diagnosed with gestational diabetes. One minute I was guiltlessly indulging in all the sweets I was craving and the next I was pushing one of those needles I dreaded into my skin three times a day to make sure that the few indulgences I allowed myself didn't put me over my prescribed glucose limits.

Then there was a fainting spell one morning on my bathroom floor (and my pregnant belly) at four o'clock, intense Braxton-Hicks contractions throughout my pregnancy, admissions to the hospital for self-induced-although-unintentional dehydration, a diagnosis of Group B Strep toward the end, and weight gain that put lots of unfamiliar and painful stress on my five-foot, two-inch frame.

In the grand scheme of things, I realize these were all teeny-tiny blips on the "poor me" scale. I survived, just like billions of other women had before me and would after me, and none of these inconveniences harmed my unborn baby in any way. It wasn't an easy thirty-six weeks, but it was a time frame I wouldn't trade for anything—ever.

With the difficulties I had throughout the pregnancy, I figured the obstetrical gods would sprinkle me with easy dust when my delivery day arrived. Let's just say I was wrong. The day we welcomed Maxwell Alston Sutter into the world was one I wouldn't wish on my worst enemy.

It was July 25, 2007. I was thirty-five weeks and six days into my pregnancy. I started the day off as I usually did— literally rolling out of bed. As the day went on, the pings on my worry radar got more and more intense. I just didn't feel right. My doctor had always told me to tune into my body's signals, and the unnatural level of nausea and intense abdominal pain told me loud and clear that I needed to get to the hospital. My doctor happened to be out of town (the *only* week that summer she had plans, of course), but I managed to reach her on the phone, and she agreed that when Ryan got home from a short bike ride, I should get checked out. As soon as he was back, we were on our way to the Vail Valley Medical Center.

The triage nurses in the emergency room determined that I needed to head upstairs to the labor and delivery department, where I was admitted immediately. The nursing staff went to work strapping a fetal monitor to my belly, taking my vitals, and ordering up blood work. My blood pressure was normally about 100/70, so when it consistently read about 135/90, the on-call doctors were a tad concerned. My blood work wasn't any better. Thankfully, the combination of all my concerning symptoms didn't require delivery at that point, but it did require an overnight stay for observation. I was more than happy to oblige, knowing I was in good hands.

When I woke up the next morning, the doctors told me I would be delivering a baby that day. Even though it wasn't unexpected given my test results, I had really hoped to go full term. In my heart of hearts, I knew that babies were more than viable at thirty-six weeks, but after having worked in the neonatal intensive care unit at Miami Children's Hospital, and knowing that the decreased oxygen levels at our Rocky Mountain altitude would impact our little peanut's lungs, I was a nervous wreck.

A nurse applied Cytotec (a drug to induce labor) and we started the waiting process for "natural" childbirth to begin.

Over the course of the day, I started showing signs of pre-eclampsia and a life-threatening complication known as HELLP syndrome, which is characterized by a low platelet count and elevated liver enzymes. When my blood work came back with these results, the medical professionals around me were having a hard time containing their anxiety. They had tried to wait for labor to kick in, but as the lab work got worse and worse, the ambiance in my room turned from semi-peaceful anticipation to frantic chaos. My failing body didn't have the luxury of time, so they handed Ryan a pair of scrubs and explained that we were heading to the operating room for a C-section. What I didn't know was that they were doing this to save my life.

I was wheeled into the OR and given an epidural in hopes that I could remain awake and Ryan could stay by my side. The doctor waited a few minutes for it to kick in and then attempted to make an incision. Big problem, though: I could feel it! With my condition growing more dire by the minute—I was in danger of falling into a coma or being wracked by seizures—the doctors couldn't wait any longer for the epidural to take effect and I was told I would be put under general anesthesia. Then the doctor turned to my husband and said, "I'm sorry, Mr. Sutter, but you'll need to wait outside."

I don't remember much that followed, but I do remember that the anesthesiologist had injected something into my IV that made it so I couldn't breathe or move, although I was still conscious. I was gripped with fear. From what I understand, they were unable to give me the drug that would ease me into unconsciousness until Ryan let go of my hand and left the room. It felt much longer than the milliseconds it took for him to leave, but when that happened, my fear finally disappeared and the surgeons did their magic.

Whether my trip to dreamland was filled with blossoming meadows or turquoise ocean views, I'll never know, but I won't forget that I never got to hear Max's first precious cry, hear the doctor happily announce, "It's a boy!" or see Ryan cut the umbilical cord. However, had my doctors not been so dedicated, educated, and quick to pull the trigger, both Max and I could very well have died that day. Instead, at 8:50 p.m., our healthy little guy came into the world, and soon after, I was able to bond with my baby boy and bask in the glow of my newly expanded family as if nothing had gone wrong.

For the next year, we focused our attention on the miracle that was our firstborn, and we would've continued that focus had we not been unexpectedly blessed so quickly with the final piece to our family puzzle: a baby girl. If only she hadn't felt the need to make her grand entrance during a storm the news stations called the "Blizzard of 2009."

At thirty-seven weeks pregnant, I had spent the previous night nervously driving around our neighborhood searching for our Siberian husky, Natasha, as Max was sound asleep with a neighbor watching guard. Tosh had escaped through our fence (for the thousandth time) and hadn't returned as she always had before. I was so stressed out that Ryan got someone to cover for him at the Vail fire station and came home to help scour the neighborhood for her. For at least an hour, he trounced through snowy yards and every open space around us searching for her tracks. No luck. Finally Ryan returned to work, and I returned to fretting.

Later that night, I learned that Tosh had been picked up by a modern-day dogcatcher and could be "rescued" in the morning. I called Ryan with the news and hit the sack.

I woke up the next day with a plan to conquer the usual tasks of life with a twenty-month-old and then head to the Humane Society to bring Natasha home. Blakesley had other plans.

Throughout the morning, I was experiencing more intense contractions than usual and a strange sensation I had never felt before. I called my doctor and she told me that I most likely had lost my mucus plug (not nearly as gross as it sounds) and needed to pack my bag and meet her at the hospital. I found a trusted friend to stay with Max and headed out into the storm with my friend Evin, who offered to take me when I explained that Ryan was stuck at work.

The problem was that in our little town, I-70 is the only road to the hospital from our house. The. Only. Road. And it passes through an area called Dowd Junction, which is constantly plagued with accidents. That day was no different. In fact, it was much worse.

After multiple cars had slid off the road, a state trooper was given orders to block further traffic from getting through. If I hadn't been told that I had to get to the hospital and known from past experience that I was in danger of developing life-threatening preeclampsia and HELLP syndrome again, we would've waited out the storm with the rest of the annoyed drivers. We would've had no choice. After talking to Ryan, though, and hearing that an ambulance behind us couldn't even get through, we knew we needed to make a move before our options disappeared into the whiteout.

As Evin pulled up to the officer, we heard lots of angry drivers behind us blaring their horns. No matter how loud it got, that noise didn't stop us. I explained the situation to the trooper. I couldn't help but feel awful for the poor man.

You could tell he was terrified and in no way ready to break out his latex-free gloves and first-aid kit. Thank goodness he didn't let his fear get in the way of his wisdom and he let us proceed.

Evin cautiously inched the car forward foot by foot, passing dozens of accidents along the way. It took us at least ten times as long as it normally does, but eventually we got past all of them and made it safely to the hospital.

Ryan met us there and was immediately given a spiffy cap and scrubs. With our team of doctors prepared for a recurrence of what had happened to me during my first delivery, we headed straight to the OR. This time, though, the spinal worked, and I was conscious the whole time. I still had to get a C-section, but I got to hear the extraordinary sound of Blakesley's first cry. I was now the *very* proud mother of two.

With thirty-six years under my belt, I had everything I had dreamed of (except maybe a closet full of Louboutins and Shop ItToMe.com outfits, Dr. Oz's phone number on speed dial, no debt, a personal chef, the ability to fly, and the angelic voice of Carrie Underwood). From then on, I knew that a daily public acknowledgment of gratitude would be a necessity in my life.

I had been introduced to the idea of acknowledging personal blessings of the day by one of my idols, Oprah Winfrey. It was the year 2000, and I had tuned in to her show after a few months in a hole of depression. That day, she encouraged viewers to take a moment every night to write down five things they were grateful for, and I took her advice. I wanted to focus on what my life was blessed with instead of what my life was missing.

Shortly after Blakesley was born, I remembered that show and decided to start a daily exercise in gratitude via my

#favepartofday posts. They didn't have to be about monumental milestones or pinch-me-I-must-be-dreaming moments, but with the help of social media, they became the way I shared the teeniest Sutters' everyday events with loved ones and friends living hundreds or thousands of miles away. They reminded me that it's the little things that matter most. They helped keep my chin up when my day was less than pleasant and continue to keep me grounded in my reality: life as a stay-at-home-and-work-full-time mom, wife, daughter, sister, and friend.

Above all else, they became a daily reminder to be grateful for all the blessed pieces of my life . . . big and small.

Perception Is Reality

Gratitude is a way of seeing, a way of being, a way of giving back. Gratefulness is part of the little, everyday things as well as the major, life-changing experiences. It affects the way the world sees us, and the way we see the world. In fact, a research study conducted by Dr. Robert Emmons, a psychology professor at the University of California–Davis, found that people who actively practice gratitude can increase their happiness levels by 25 percent.

Being grateful isn't just about acknowledging the obvious blessings. It should also be about seeing positive value that may be hidden from the surface.

Imagine a messy living room strewn with child-size dump trucks that have taken loads of toys to the landfill (otherwise known as the couch). If that were my home, and it often is, the pessimist in me would focus on the fact that as soon as I tidy up the mess, the kids and I will most likely be right back down on the floor putting everything away again later that day. What a waste of time!

As William James, a psychologist and author, once said, "The greatest discovery of my generation is that human beings can alter their lives by altering their attitudes of mind." By choosing an optimistic attitude, I am able to see the exact same living room in an entirely different light. In forcing myself to look past the superficial layer of chaos, I am shown a much deeper meaning of abundance and joy. That messy living room is a testament that healthy, happy, energetic children live in a home full of things they love, with people they love and imaginations that can take them anywhere.

Recognizing what lies beneath a dull task can turn it into an expression of appreciation, if we just remember to see the world with a grateful heart.

Don't get me wrong—I have days when the bright side is not on my radar and I would rather wallow in my bad mood.

I did it when my parents got divorced.

I did it when my cousin died at a young age.

I did it when Alex broke my heart.

Sometimes you just have to let sadness or anger or frustration into your present to eventually put it in the past. But be careful not to let those feelings linger.

Had I been the one to receive the final rose, I may have been spared lots of sleepless nights and even more tears after my initial heartbreak, but Ryan and I probably never would have met and the trajectory of my life wouldn't have included Maxwell Alston or Blakesley Grace Sutter. The mere thought that they might never have existed sends shivers down my spine. It also makes me that much more thankful for my heartache. From the bottom of my heart, thank you, Alex Michel.

These days I allow myself to feel the pain, but not to immerse myself in it. I try to get past it as quickly as I can and get on with the good stuff. As Alex Tan, a political activist from Singapore, once said, "Perhaps our eyes need to be washed by our tears once in a while, so that we can see life with a clearer view again."

By recognizing my daily blessings, I consciously know that I have much to be grateful for. I have much to get out of bed for and smile for and keep chugging along for.

We all do.

SHINE YOUR LIGHT

According to a report in the *Wall Street Journal,* being grateful gives us increased energy, optimism, social connections, and happiness. Depression, envy, greed, and addiction take a backseat when gratitude gets behind the wheel. And who doesn't want to earn more money, sleep better, fend off infection, and live with more smiles?

If you're anything like me, you want to be happy. You want to take care of the people around you. You want to make the world, especially your little sliver of it, a better place.

If you're a realist like me, however, you also know that's a tall order. "Happy" isn't something you can just order off a dinner menu. Taking care of people is a lot of work. And making the world a better place? Sometimes I feel like I'm too tired to yawn.

So where do we start? How do we change the world while we're changing diapers, trying to stay fit, putting in long hours at the office, making sure our family is well fed, and getting everyone's socks squeaky clean?

A Conscious Choice

What I've learned is that all these things—personal happiness, a stronger community, a better world—can and should be accomplished one thought at a time, one word at a time, one action so minor it may go unnoticed at a time. We can't light up the whole world, each of us, every minute, but we can decide to project optimism and light instead of pessimism and darkness. Our actions, words, and attitudes have a sizeable impact. They can either open the floodgates of global happiness or destroy our planet, one human feeling at a time.

Think about the last time someone smiled at you. Did you smile back, at least inside? Did that simple positive gesture make you want to pay it forward?

How about the last time someone was rude to you? Did it dampen your mood and make you feel like giving it right back to them in spades? It's human instinct to want to make the person who hurt you hurt even worse, especially if their insensitivity or cruelty was for no good reason.

What I have a hard time with, personally, are the unnecessary criticisms that come from cowards who anonymously hide behind their computers. I've seen comments about me like, "Dammit Trista Sutter is fugly. WTF happened to her? Motherhood? Dang," or "I think she's a disgusting mother," or this all-time favorite, "Ryan dump that broad, a garbage can would do you better." I'm usually reminded by sweet supporters (including my husband, family, and friends) that the haters are just that . . . people filled with hate. They don't know me, and most important, they don't deserve my attention. I will admit, though, that they're hard to ignore.

More valuable than the temporary satisfaction I would get from seeing these meanies brought to some kind of justice is the lesson I've learned. This quote by minister Harry

Emerson Fosdick describes it perfectly: "Hating people is like burning down your own house to get rid of a rat." Their nasty comments made me want to react. I wanted to hurt them as deeply as they had hurt me. By doing that, though, I wouldn't have made anything better. In fact, I would've hurt myself by giving in to the darkness and added fuel to their bully fire.

Now I try to hurl humor and virtual hugs instead of wallops and insults. On social media, I try to act and react with words that speak to objective facts and not subjective opinions, especially when it comes to people's physical appearance or sacred relationships.

Am I perfect? Of course not. I have moments of weakness on Twitter when it's easy to let my diarrhea of the mouth seep through in a post. (Sorry . . . disturbing visual.)

We are all allowed our bad days, but hopefully the good ones far outnumber the bad and the bad aren't bad enough to cause pain.

If you want to live in a joyful world, an easy place to start is in your own life. By recognizing that gratefulness leads to more gratitude, graciousness leads to more grace, and appreciation leads to more appreciating, we add microcosms of goodness to our universe.

If you are light, you have the potential to create more light. As teacher Erin Majors said, "A candle loses nothing by lighting another candle."

Amazing Grace

On the happiness wheel of life, there are many moving parts. Everyone has a unique wheel, dependent on their values, priorities, morals, and dreams, but without the necessary elements of gratitude and grace, the wheel can have a difficult time turning.

Clearly a book titled *Happily Ever After: The Life-Changing Power of a Grateful Heart* would indicate that gratitude is essential to happiness, but you may wonder why grace is necessary. In the most difficult of times, gratitude and its path to happiness would be blanketed by darkness if not for the light of grace.

Here's a story describing just that, a story I first heard from my friend Ethan Zohn. With a portion of his winnings as sole survivor on *Survivor: Africa,* Ethan started an organization called Grassroot Soccer that promotes HIV/AIDS education throughout Africa. He met the Biehl family through his charity work, and I'm personally thankful he did so that I would come to know their story.

Amy Biehl was a twenty-six-year-old graduate of Stanford University who traveled to South Africa to study in Cape Town as a Fulbright Scholar. Her goal: end apartheid, or at least be part of the solution. On August 25, 1993, she was driving a friend home to the Gugulethu township when she encountered a group of four enraged African men. They saw the pale color of her skin and pelted her car with bricks and rocks, eventually breaking her windshield and violently hitting her in the head. They proceeded to drag her from her car as she begged for her life. They stoned her and stabbed her and ignored her desperate pleas for mercy. They did not stop until she was dead.

Those men were the exact contradiction of grace, or "undeserved mercy," as a friend of mine once defined it. The Biehls, however, became its true personification.

Although the perpetrators were sentenced to eighteen years in prison, they were each pardoned by South Africa's Truth and Reconciliation Commission and set free after only four short years. At the hearing, not only did Amy's father, Peter Biehl, shake the hands of the men who had brutally murdered his daughter, but he stood up and said, "The most important vehicle of reconciliation is open and honest dialogue. We are here to reconcile a human life which was taken without an opportunity for dialogue. When we are finished with this process, we must move forward with linked arms." And move forward they did, not only with linked arms, but also with hearts full of grace.

They believed so much in Amy's work in South Africa that they started the Amy Biehl Foundation (AmyBiehl.org), which gives back to the very community that her killers called home. And to top that off, they forgave Ntobeko Peni and Mzikhona "Easy" Nofemela, two of her attackers (the others deciding to live a life of continued destruction), hiring them to work for the foundation and give back in Amy's name.

As reported by CNN in December 2004, Amy's mother, Linda, said, "Doing justice to Amy's legacy requires not just addressing her murderers, but also the inequalities, emotions, and difficulties that motivated Amy to help people such as Peni. He's a part of a very positive society in South Africa, raising a two-year-old child to participate in a multiethnic, multigender society. To me, that's a great joy and happiness. I've been privileged to have that opportunity."

I cannot imagine a better story of grace. A story that perfectly illustrates how deciding to live in light and unconditionally offer forgiveness can truly allow us to open the doorway to gratitude and eventual happiness. As psychiatrist Elisabeth

Kübler-Ross once said, "People are like stained-glass windows. They sparkle and shine when the sun is out, but when the darkness sets in, their true beauty is revealed only if there is light from within."

Never having met or spoken to the Biehls, I don't personally know them, but after discovering their story, I know their example of a pure and beautiful inner light is one I will never forget.

THANK YOU, PLEASE?

Whatever your name, title, or reputation, the contributions you make in your life probably don't always make front-page news or earn a Nobel Prize. They may not even come up during conversations at the dinner table or result in a simple pat on the back. In fact, they may end up being entirely overlooked. Does that mean they don't matter? Of course not! They matter. *You* matter.

As I am a stay-at-home-and-work mom, my life is filled with completing tasks that often go unnoticed. Is it my job? Yes. But just because it's a "job" doesn't mean that praise or prizes for little successes aren't more than welcome.

Everyone deserves admiration and validation, whether your day entailed doing three loads of laundry, paying the bills, and playing Candy Land or you heroically saved a woman on the brink of cardiac arrest and then got a family to safety after their car spun out of control in the middle of a blizzard.

A big celebration or a trip to your favorite jewelry store may be warranted during extra-special victories, but shockingly enough, I would take a bushel of the little things over a lavish gift any day of the week and twice on Sunday. To me, the jolt of positive energy I get when my husband reaches out to hold my hand or considerately makes me a cup of chai tea because he knows my mommy brain could use the help while I work is what gets me through the daily grind—and I need all the help I can get!

Will I cherish the lavish mama-bear necklace from Vail's Golden Bear that Ryan bought me as a "push present" after Blakesley was born? Always!

Will I forever remember how he whisked me away on a surprise trip to the Grand Tetons without my having to do anything but pack? That I will. But the things I'll remember most are the simple yet thoughtful cards he gave me leading up to and during our adventure.

Without the little things, I wouldn't have the staircase I need to reach the big things. I just need to be careful to not expect too much. What I may appreciate in terms of acclaim or reward may not be a very practical or customary expression of thanks for the people in my life.

Take my kids, for example. They are usually very sweet and loving, but as a preschooler and kindergartener, they don't have the capacity in their still-developing brains to fully grasp the efforts behind the commonplace occurrences in their lives. It may look like *Fox in Socks* by Dr. Seuss is a breeze to get through or that the smiley faces created out of the food on their lunch plates just happened by chance, but that's not the case—at least in our house. I could very easily choose a book without sixty-one pages of tongue-twisters (parents: you should try it! It's not easy) to read them at bedtime or dish up their lunchtime eats in a nondescript way, but where's the fun in that? It definitely takes a little more effort, but feeding their minds and their bodies is not only my job, it's my pleasure. Hopefully, someday giving compliments will be second nature to them, and I may hear "good job, Mommy" or "thank you for the thoughtful touch, Mom" without encouragement from their dad. Until then (or until they're too cool for their mother's cutesy ways), the pride I get from the resulting ear-to-ear grins that splash across their faces will be enough.

And to be clear, it's not that I dream of constant, around-the-clock acknowledgment. I can't even imagine how annoying it would be if Ryan followed me around everywhere thanking me for picking up a fallen sticker or wiping off a spot on the refrigerator door handle. Authentic appreciation is one thing. Obligatory appreciation is another. Not only would I go bonkers, but the sincerity of any gratitude I could receive would be diluted and felt as though it was expressed just for the sake of expression. I would rather feel genuinely appreciated while performing everyday tasks and in more exceptional moments than disingenuously recognized for everything under the sun.

So, go out, watch, and listen for that fine line of praise. Appreciate the little things, celebrate the big things, and know that you matter.

Say It Forward

"I appreciate you."

It's one of the most profound things someone can say to you. If you've ever heard the words, and I hope you have, you know what it feels like. It's a warm smile from within . . . no force required. It means you matter, that your existence is a blessing—and there is no better feeling than that. Mother

Teresa said it best: "There is more hunger for love and appreciation in this world than for bread."

I truly understood the importance of genuine expressions of thanks when I came face-to-face with the idea that my former manager considered me an unappreciative mooch. I was at the Lodge at Rancho Mirage in Palm Springs, California, where I was counting down the handful of days left until I exchanged vows with the man of my dreams. Getting ready for the night's festivities, I had the television tuned to *Entertainment Tonight*. I heard my name, but not in a complimentary way. The speaker was a famous lawyer I had never met, and he was on national television bashing me in front of millions of people watching at home.

To make a long story short, the man I had trusted to act as my manager felt he was entitled to a larger commission than what we had verbally agreed to in regard to the compensation Ryan and I would receive to have our wedding televised. I disagreed, paid him what he had agreed to over the phone, and ended our managerial relationship. I then found out during a taping of *Larry King Live,* two days before this lawyer's appearance on *ET,* that he was suing me. With only a verbal agreement between us, I resentfully prepared myself to go through the motions and hired a lawyer of my own.

In a suit I later filed with the California labor commissioner, I successfully proved that he wasn't entitled to any more of my earnings and, in fact, owed me money, but that was months down the road. Days before what was to be the happiest day of my life, this fancy attorney wasn't only insinuating that I owed my former manager money, but he decided to add insult to injury and call me ungrateful. The dagger in my heart was almost too much to bear.

Having been in the public eye for several years at that point, I knew I could handle a lot of name-calling, but for someone to say that I was anything but appreciative destroyed me, and I have a feeling my ex-manager knew it would.

The lawyer mentioned that my former manager had gone above and beyond the call of duty in arranging for me to temporarily call Beverly Hills home when I first arrived, and that when my time there came to an end, I hadn't given him even the courtesy of a thank-you. I thought, "This guy is lying to America!" and I hated him for it. But even though I was convinced that he couldn't be telling the truth, I couldn't help but wonder: Had I actually done what he was so frustratingly accusing me of? Had I failed to profusely thank my manager and the owner of the house that I had been housesitting for helping provide me with such an appreciated opportunity? There was no way . . . or was there?

I had always known how important it is to be vocal about being thankful, but this experience etched the lesson so deeply in my skull that I would be forever changed. As the composer and producer Bernice Johnson Reagon said, "Life's challenges are not supposed to paralyze you, they're supposed to help you discover who you are." From that day forward, I knew who I wanted to be: a woman who was so outwardly grateful that no one could ever question it. If I was ever on the receiving end of a kindness or generosity, I would do my best to take the time and effort to literally and liberally say thank you both in person and by way of simple and sincere notes or gifts of gratitude.

When the time came, our wedding went off without a hitch (although I could've done without the helicopters!), but I will never forget the accusations. After that experience, I'll always remember that if you don't say thank you loud enough, people remember . . . and they tell other people. In my case, lots and lots of other people.

Expressing your gratitude isn't an extra. It's everything.

But as is the case with most things in life, how you say thank you is less about the size of the gesture and more about its quality.

Appreciation can be as loud as the winning team's cheering section at a football game or as subtle as the glimmer in the eye of a baby getting swaddled after a warm bath. My personal favorite expression of appreciation is a hug (yes, I'm a hugger). I'm also a fan of the old-school tradition of writing formal thank-you notes, even if it takes me months to do so (and it usually does). After all, thank-you notes aren't just pretty pieces of paper full of meaningless writing. They are symbols of appreciation that put gratitude into words.

For example, take the card that Ryan gave me for our eighth wedding anniversary. The outside said, "What Would I Do Without You?" The inside:

> Angel, Happy Anniversary! Thank you for being the rock that stands as the foundation of our marriage and the glue that holds our family together. The amount of love you possess is humbling to me. I am lucky to have some of that love and appreciate your willingness to love "all" of me, the good and bad, through both easy and hard times. You are a truly special person, a perfect mom, and a beautiful wife. Thank you for being my wife! I love you! Forever & ever & ever & ever . . . Ryan

We do say "I love you" and "thank you" when it comes to doing the dishes or taking out the trash, but it's nice to have his heartfelt appreciation in a way that I can carry with me everywhere.

Remember how it feels to be validated by the words "I appreciate you," and say it forward. If we can all remember to appreciate one another, we will all shine a little brighter. Poet and author Maya Angelou's words on the topic say it all: "People will forget what you said, people will forget what you did, but people will never forget how you made them feel."

HAPPILY EVER ACTIONS

~ Start up a gratitude journal. Set aside time each day, whether it is bedtime or during your lunch break or as you sip on your morning java, to formally acknowledge through the written word one to five things you are grateful for. There are no wrong entries.

~ Close your eyes and think of the best parts of your life. It could be as small as the beating of your heart or as all-encompassing as the memories of a happy childhood. Open your mind, let your imagination run wild, and focus on this quote by author Sarah Ban Breathnach: "All we have is all we need. All we need is the awareness of how blessed we really are."

~ If your day is rotten, stop what you are doing, grab paper and a pen, and let your stream of consciousness guide your hands in counting your blessings, thereby canceling out the negativity surrounding you. Put those thoughts in your pocket or your purse and carry them with you as you return to your newly brightened day.

≈ Too busy to grab paper and pen? Just take a moment to breathe and think about one thing you're grateful for.

≈ Remember the basics: treat people how you would like to be treated. Living by the Golden Rule isn't always easy, especially when you throw feelings and life stressors into the mix, but if there is a lifestyle you can be proud of living, that's the one.

Feel GREATful:
The Art of Appreciating
and Nurturing Yourself

Give thanks for what you are now, and keep
fighting for what you want to be tomorrow.

—FERNANDA MIRAMONTES-LANDEROS

"YOU CAN'T INVITE YOUR FRIENDS AND LOVED ONES inside of a house you haven't built yet." Rev Run, the hip-hop legend and minister, definitely has a way with words, and when he posted this quote on Twitter, I immediately wrote it in the little journal I have dedicated to collecting my favorites. It was the perfect way to describe two notions that have guided the most important relationships of my life: (1) It is only through knowing and truly loving yourself that you can ever welcome anyone else into your world; (2) It is only by taking care of your personal health and well-being that you will have the energy and ability to care for the people who depend on you, including your kids, spouse, parents, friends, or even your precious babies with fur or feathers.

If you've ever been on an airplane, you've heard the safety announcements: "In the unlikely event of pressure loss, oxygen masks will appear overhead. If you are seated next to a small child or someone needing assistance, secure your own mask first before assisting them."

Until I became a mother, that sounded so selfish to me. You shouldn't offer help to those who need it most before you take care of yourself? That's not what all those lessons of childhood taught me! I should be a giving person, right?

Someone who puts others before herself, right? After all, if I don't place the oxygen mask on the little faces of those depending on me, who will? Well, no one if I've already lost consciousness (God forbid!). The only way to ensure that they have what they need is to make sure that I can give them what they need—and that means taking care of myself first.

This is not to say that you are more important than those you are caring for, but that you are *as* important. Just because you've dedicated your life, or your flight, or the past few years to caring for someone less independent than you doesn't mean that you deserve any less of a life yourself. You are worthy. You deserve love. You deserve appreciation.

Whether you give back to yourself in the form of an annual trip with just your buddies or a nightly veg session on the couch with your guilty pleasure on the tube is up to you. Just remember not to forget the person in your life who needs you more than anyone: you. That is anything but selfish.

FILL 'ER UP!

We all have an appreciation tank that needs filling. The more validation we get, the happier and more fulfilled we feel, allowing us to travel through life with an immense sense of confidence, pleasure, and positivity. Those we receive from our friends, family, hobbies, and job successes can be a wonderful addition to the foundation we've built for ourselves. The beauty, though, is that we need nothing more than self-love to fill the tank all the way to the top. As the American author Louis L'Amour once said, "I need nobody to make me somebody."

Filling our tanks is a constant process. Unless we want to stay on empty, remain stagnant, and let the beauty of this life happen to other people, we need to actively appreciate the unique blessings that we are. Whether it's on a daily, weekly, or annual basis, doing things for ourselves is something that needs to happen to keep us feeling like worthy owners of a chunk of the world's happiness. Besides, if we constantly give to the other people and things in our lives, we will end up resenting them unless we've also given some to ourselves.

There are millions of ways we can show self-love—it's just up to us to know what will give us the most bang for the buck, and to find a balance between too much and too little, inspiring and discouraging, wise and foolish, self-centered and altruistic, right and wrong. A glass of red wine after the kids go to bed may be just what you need to perk up your mood, but if you'll find satisfaction only when the bottle costs upward of $1,500 and you have debt up the wazoo, you may need to rethink your personal validation strategy.

To help get the expressive juices of gratitude flowing, I enlisted a few friends to share their favorite ways to fill up their tanks. I think you'll love what they came up with as much as I do.

- My friend and once-upon-a-time fellow coworker Tracey Moses said this: "I blast the music and simply dance around the house. And I mean *blare* it!"

  As Vicki Baum, an Austrian writer, once said, "There are short-cuts to happiness, and dancing is one of them." Even without rhythm or coordination, getting the wiggles out does a body, and a mind, good—and there's heaps of research to prove it. Study after study reports mood improvement, stress relief, increased self-confidence, diminished depression, better health, and greater energy levels, even if it's done in the privacy of your own home. I'd say that's a perfect way to move the appreciation-tank meter up.

- Nathalie McNeil, one of my friends from Miami Children's Hospital, told me she'd been doing some of Deepak Chopra's 21-day Meditation Challenges. "I started them because I have a hard time winding down to go to bed and have read about the documented benefits of decreasing anxiety and relaxation. It definitely helps me fall asleep faster, which results in more sleep and a better mood the next day."

  Nathalie is as honest as they come, but you don't have to take her word about the benefits. The world of science has been investigating this practice for years, and many studies have shown that meditation can decrease stress levels, induce calm, manage chronic pain, and improve brain function. In addition, one recent study, published in November 2012, found that transcendental meditation significantly reduced the risk of stroke, heart attack, and mortality in people suffering from coronary heart disease.

  With many different types and elements, there are possibilities out there for everyone—it's all about finding the right fit for you. And don't worry about breaking out your credit cards. Meditation can be done anywhere at any time. It could be just what you need to keep your engine running on happy.

- My fellow mountain mama Allie Cross told me, "I throw myself parties! I am past the stage of wedding showers (married ten years) and baby showers (two kids) but

I still love to celebrate. Last year I rented a big party bike and treated all my friends to a tour of downtown Denver—complete with party favors and everything. It was all for me. I am already planning this year's celebration and my friends have totally gotten on board and started to plan events for themselves too. Next month a bunch of us are going roller skating with a friend who planned her own party. We are all having so much fun!"

I bet! I actually started talking about doing something similar with my Vail friends after my fortieth birthday party in 2012. It was truly one of the most fun nights of my life and I decided that I would love to re-create it every year, but not with any particular guest of honor. My vision is to have one big blowout birthday bash to celebrate everyone all at once. After hearing from Allie, though, I'm thinking more frequent get-togethers throughout the year are the way to do it. I *love* this idea and its potential for profound investment in each of our appreciation tanks.

- While we were out to dinner with one of our friends, Bernard David, who is always inspiring and insightful, he told me of a friend of his who attends laughing groups. Yes, he said laughing groups.

I had heard of groups that laugh, of course, but groups that specifically got together to do only that . . . never. I soon found LaughterYoga.org, and after clicking on the video on their home page, I couldn't help but smile and laugh right along with the giggly people on my computer screen. Started in India in 1995 as a complete well-being workout, these gatherings are based on the scientific fact that the body can't differentiate between real and fake laughter, and when we laugh, we get happy and more joyful. As the American philosopher William James is quoted as saying, "We don't laugh because we're happy—we're happy because we laugh." I asked my Twitter followers if any of them had ever attended one. Nickie George responded, "OMG yes and it was better than 2 years of therapy!!!" Even without ever meeting Nickie or knowing her story, her tweet was enough to convince me that an organized group of strangers doing nothing but laughing could flood all of our tanks with happy juice.

- My college friend David Liberatore had this to share: "I work very hard, so I make sure to PLAY very hard. You only live once . . . so I make sure I take vacations whenever possible, even if it's just a weekend of skiing in Vermont or a 3-day visit to South Florida. Spoil yourself if you deserve it. Traveling (experiencing new places and new adventures) is what I do to treat myself for all the hard work I do."

As you should, Dave. As we all should!

SO MANY CHOICES

You make hundreds of decisions in a day. Should I brown-bag it or order a Double Quarter Pounder with cheese, extra-large fries, and a Triple Thick chocolate shake for lunch? Should I wear a white T-shirt and jeans or my ever-so-comfy sweats? Should I listen to Bruno Mars or Miranda Lambert? Should I this? Should I that? Should I? Should I? Should I?

Life is certainly filled with lots of choices, but the ones that truly matter affect the big picture—the ones you make with each breath you take. They determine your attitude, outlook, legacy, and integrity.

In every moment of every day, you can either choose to accept your circumstances with a smile, be thankful, and strive toward happiness, or choose to sit back with a scowl succumbing to self-doubt and not fully appreciating that you are here to live your own unique life. A life that may not be full of daily roses and fairy tales, but a precious life that is yours to live . . . yours to experience . . . yours to mold and shape and appreciate.

Whether you feel good, bad, or somewhere in between, you have the ability to accentuate your time on earth through the power of thought—making it better, worse, or drearily indifferent. As Mother Teresa once said, "There is no key to happiness. The door is always open." All it takes is forward motion over the threshold. To take that step, you have to harness the power of your mind, guiding it in the direction of your life's bliss. It may not seem easy, but if a seventy-five-year-old man, exhausted from tip to toe, can do it, I have a feeling that you can too.

Let me explain.

It was October 16, 2004, and my husband of almost one year had just finished his first attempt at the formidable Ironman World Championship in Kona, Hawaii. With a smile across his face, he finished his third triathlon ever, in a respectable eleven hours and thirty-eight minutes. After getting showered with congratulations from the group of friends and family (me included, of course!) who had joined us on the big island, refueling at Kona Style Fish 'n' Chips, and taking what was likely one of the most satisfying showers of his life, we returned to the bleachers at the finish line with about an hour to spare before the race officially ended. It was late and Ryan had fatigued his body like never before, but he decided to put his much-needed rest on hold for what we had been told would be the most inspiring part of our Ironman experience, and I'm so glad we did.

Sitting among hundreds of others, Ryan and I anxiously awaited the participants who were striving to finish before the strict cutoff time. I was prepared to be heartbroken for those who didn't make it by midnight, but I wasn't prepared to actually see the human mind in action right before my very eyes.

I'll never forget it.

Bib #200 was approaching the archway that he'd had in his sights for over 16 1/2 hours; he was literally running diagonal to the ground. Though the miles he'd traveled and the minutes he'd suffered had begun to alter the way his body functioned, he wasn't letting that stop him. He was going to make it across. He had already made the choice, no matter how badly he hurt or how tired he was.

At sixteen hours, forty-five minutes, and fifty-four seconds, a man in his seventies crossed the finish line, and with his very next step, he collapsed into the arms of a volunteer. He had exhausted the perceived limits of his body, finishing the race with the remarkable strength of his will. Accomplishing his goal to finish, his mind relaxed its supportive grip on his weary muscles as they collapsed into a heap of satisfaction and accomplishment.

I have never met him, but I was touched by his incredible display of determination and willpower. He had a choice and he chose to cross that finish line. He chose to achieve his goal. He chose to leave a lasting impression on all who urged him under the final Ironman archway.

Mahatma Gandhi once said, "Strength does not come from physical capacity. It comes from an indomitable will."

When this man chose to train, compete, finish, and not give up on what was surely one of the most grueling days of his seventy-five years, he demonstrated an indomitable will. He exemplified the tremendous capacity of the human spirit that exists within each of us. We are all capable of summoning the powers of our mind to help us push through pain, grow through adversity, and appreciate the beauty we see in even our most challenging times.

Only one person can choose how you respond to adversity and how you live your life. It's not your mother or your father, your brother, your boss, or your kids. It's you.

You are your conscious thought. You have control. Take it. Own it. Live it.

THE NEGATIVES AND THE POSITIVES

On MathIsFun.com, students learning basic math are told, "Subtracting a negative is the same as adding." If only people in the midst of negativity could take themselves back to elementary school math and apply that lesson to their lives, they could embrace this piece of common wisdom: "Every time you subtract negative from your life, you make room for more positive." To remove negativity, though, you must first acknowledge that it exists. As journalist Oliver Burkeman stated in a 2012 *New York Times* article titled "The Power of Negative Thinking," by deliberately visualizing the worst-case scenario, you usually conclude that you can cope.

However, allowing a negative thought to momentarily enter to keep us safe from harm is one thing. Allowing negative thoughts to persistently dominate our psyche and destroy our self-respect is another. So other than scheduling regular sessions with a licensed psychological expert, how do we overcome those nasty little notions and maximize our happiness level?

After doing a little research, I found a really interesting three-part study coauthored by Richard Petty, a psychology professor at Ohio State University. In the first part, the scientists showed that if you want to free your mind of a negative thought, you need to literally throw it out. They started by asking eighty-three high school students to write down a positive or negative thought about their body. After three minutes, they were all asked to reflect on what they wrote. Half of them were then told to throw their written thought in the trash and the other half were told to check for any grammatical mistakes and hold on to their piece of paper. Next, everyone rated their attitudes toward their bodies.

The results showed that for those who kept what they wrote down, their ratings were directly influenced by whether their written thought was positive or negative. If they had initially written something positive, their positive attitude was accentuated. If they wrote something negative, that too was accentuated. On the flip side, for those who trashed their recorded thought, their attitudes weren't affected by what they first thought of their bodies. In fact, their first thought wasn't even a blip on their radar, whether negative or positive.

In the second part of their study, Petty et al. asked a different set of 284 students what they thought about the Mediterranean diet. They separated them into three groups: those who threw their thoughts away, those who kept them on their desk, and those who protected their thoughts by keeping them in their purse or wallet. As in the first part, Richard Petty said, "Those who kept the list of thoughts at their desk were more influenced by them when evaluating the diet than were those who threw them away. However, those who protected their thoughts by putting them in a pocket or purse were even more influenced than those who kept the thoughts on their desk."

He went on to say that the second experiment suggested that "you can magnify your thoughts, and make them more important to you, by keeping them with you in your wallet or purse."

"At some level, it can sound silly. But we found that it really works—by physically throwing away or protecting your thoughts, you influence how you end up using those thoughts," said Petty. "Of course, even if you throw the thoughts in a garbage can or put them in the recycle bin on the computer, they are not really gone—you can regenerate them. But the representations of those thoughts are gone, at least temporarily, and it seems to make it easier to not think about them. Your body can control your mind, just as your mind controls your body."

How cool is that? Treat your thoughts like material objects and do with them what you will. Trash or treasure—it's up to you.

IMPERFECTLY PERFECT

Learning to embrace the not-so-perfect-you and the mistakes you've made along the way can be just as important as acknowledging the everyday things that deserve merit. Just as the pianist Vladimir Horowitz once said, "Perfection itself is imperfection."

For most of my childhood, I was a pretty good kid, but I do vividly remember one bump in the road. The day still sticks out "like a sore butt."

I was seven or eight years old, playing at my neighbor Nikki's house. Before I headed home, I decided that her lipstick, seashells, and a school picture of our shared babysitter deserved to be mine, so I stuffed them in my bag. My memory is a little foggy about the details of how my parents found out about my sticky fingers, but I do remember that they forced me back across the street to look my friend in the eye, apologize, and return all her cherished goodies. Afterward, my dad introduced me to what a belt felt like against my backside—oh yes, a good old-fashioned lesson on the consequences of theft.

I had been spanked before, but the belt opened my eyes to a whole new world of hurt, and I was not a fan. Couple that with the profound disappointment I saw in my parents' eyes, and my life of crime was over (at least until I turned sixteen and had my first unsupervised date with peppermint schnapps). I couldn't bear that look, and from that day forward, I was pretty much branded a rule follower. I knew that if I made my parents happy, I would be happy—in theory, at least.

Looking back, I can laugh at how I was so pathetic at being naughty that I actually chose lipstick, common seashells, and a picture the size of a cracker to establish myself as a badass. From where I stand now, I can also appreciate my naïveté and know that my punishment was necessary to teach me right from wrong. I wasn't too keen on it at the time, and don't know that I will do the same as a mom if my little buggers go down a path of thievery, but I know my parents cared enough to set me straight, and for that I am one lucky square peg.

Although I will continue to strive toward perfection, I will always appreciate the imperfections that helped mold me into the person I am today. I may not be able to change the past, but I can try to make the future better for having lived it.

GOING TO EXTREMES

In December 2011, I was asked to be part of a photo shoot that would end up on the cover of *In Touch Weekly* in January 2012. Smiling alongside me in their just-as-itsy bikinis would be two of the beauties who had also been given the once-in-a-lifetime opportunity as *The Bachelorette*: Ashley Hebert and Ali Fedotowsky. I was honored that I had even been considered because, next to them, I was no spring chicken.

During my interview with the writer from the magazine, we joked about my "maturity" and how my impending fortieth birthday was affecting my body image. Without a thought as to how it would be conveyed to readers, I poked fun at the gravitational changes that were showing themselves a bit more obviously than they had in years past. I laughed at the deflated water balloons that occupied my chest after nursing two children for a year each, the veins that were appearing on the backs of my legs, the impact my sun-worshipping days were having on my face, and the scoreboard that showed genetics winning out over the elasticity of my right eyelid.

When the issue showed up in our local grocery store, the captions under the picture on the cover told anyone walking by that the other girls were focused on fitness. Mine shouted out that Trista had "plans for a boob job and Botox"!

I was horrified.

Yes, I had joked about it with the writer, but to me the cover insinuated that I was gung ho about going under the knife and couldn't wait to beat Heidi Montag's record number of surgical procedures performed in one day. That couldn't have been further from the truth.

Before that shoot, I never thought of myself as someone who wanted, needed, or would even consider what seemed like extreme methods to change my appearance back into someone I wasn't anymore or to something it had never been in the first place. To each his own, but I never thought it would be for me.

I had supported friends who had chosen to undergo cosmetic procedures and envied celebrities who were "aging gracefully," but I didn't think I'd have the guts or the desire to ever go there. Like I said earlier, I am deathly afraid of needles and, more important, I have kids for whom I hope to always be a positive role model, especially when it comes to my daughter and her body image. In my mind, plastic surgery was painful, always criticized, and anything but positive.

On the flip side, though, lack of self-confidence and not trying to be the best possible version of yourself aren't all that great either. I didn't want Max and Blakesley to witness my seeds of doubt, and they had certainly been watered enough inside of me to start taking over our household garden soon. What was right and what was wrong?

After the story hit newsstands, my insecurities became very real and no longer just the butt of my "I'm getting old" jokes. The printed words really hit me. As fate would have it, they also made an impression on a prominent plastic surgeon in Houston.

Dr. Franklin Rose, the father of my fellow *Bachelor* alumna Erica Rose, had performed thousands of mommy makeovers. Erica told me that her father had said that if I was serious about looking into my options, he would be happy to speak with me. We scheduled an initial chat, and then another, and then quite a few more. I got advice from people I knew who had been through procedures, as well as from those who hadn't but knew all about my insecurities. I spent months contemplating the pros and cons and discussing them with my husband and close friends, who I knew would love me no matter what I decided.

It was a battle between the inner demons that teased me every time I looked at myself in the mirror or in a photo, and those that reminded me that not only do I have an intense fear of sharp objects but that I would be up against some pretty harsh critics. One little voice inside said, "Go for it!" and the other said, "You are nuts!"

Ultimately my inner realist convinced me that what truly mattered was how I felt about myself. As Shireen Haiderali said, "The world doesn't have to think you are beautiful, but you do." She was right. With the medical technology and training of the doctors of today, I could correct a genetically drooping eyelid and through breast augmentation and an internal lift get back the full breasts I had been endowed with for most of my adult life.

Did my decision mean that I wasn't proud of my heritage (my mom has the same droopy eye)? Not in the least.

It also didn't mean that I, for even one millisecond, regretted sacrificing my body to provide my children with the most natural form of nourishment on the planet. My body was created to breast-feed (among other things) and I was honored that I was able to share that incredibly precious time with my babies, kick-starting their immune systems and bonding with them in such a special way.

With my heart convinced that it was the best decision for me, I scheduled my surgery for July 18, booked my round-trip flight to Houston, and spent the weeks leading up to it stockpiling hugs and gathering reassurances that I wouldn't regret my decision.

The surgery went "perfectly," per Dr. Rose, but I beat myself up for weeks afterward. I let the fear of judgment cloud my reality for a while. I tried to beat my naysayers to the punch by criticizing myself for what I had done, wallowing in pain and guilt. However, I had the unconditional support of my family and friends and, in time, saw through that dark cloud.

Ultimately I learned that outer beauty is (as they say) in the eye of the beholder. I am pretty sure that I will continue to have days of self-doubt, and that's okay, but I will always try to rise above my demons and focus on the parts of my body that I tend to invest more pride in.

I made a decision to correct a couple of my physical in-securities, and no matter what anyone said or says, I won't let that decision define me. I am the one who has to look at myself in the mirror, and now that things are settling into position, I am grateful that the dominoes of this story fell as they did. With a little help from the trained hands of a plastic surgeon, I was able to smile more confidently than I had in years. In a world full of highlights and lowlights, padded bras, eyelash curlers and lengthening mascaras, facials, moistur-izers, tanning salons, acrylic nails, and the genius invention of Spanx, we all are just trying to look and feel our best. I could've done without the scalpels and pain, but for me the "extreme" decision was the right decision.

As William Shakespeare said, "To thine own self be true, and it must follow, as the night the day, thou canst not then be false to any man."

HAPPILY EVER ACTIONS

≈ In your own personal quest for happiness, remember that you don't have to search far. As Iyanla Vanzant, an inspirational speaker, has said, "Joy is not what happens to you; it is what comes through you when you are conscious of the blessing you are." Each night, reflect on one thing you appreciate about yourself. You can write it down or keep it stored away in the archives of your mind—it's up to you—but just do it, and be ready to feel the joy.

≈ Have a brainstorming session with yourself about the not-so-favorite parts of yourself. Maybe it's your penchant for snacking or the shape of your eyebrows, your split ends or the fact that you haven't talked to your mom in two weeks. Hone in on one thing that you can easily change (for example, picking up the phone and dialing your mom's number just because or going through your pantry and throwing your go-to snacks in the garbage) and get to work, but not for anyone but yourself.

≈ Indulge in an old-fashioned dose of "me time." Take inspiration from the examples of my friends, or do as I do and veg on the couch, indulge in a little retail therapy (with a budget), or head to your local nail salon. Something as simple as freshly polished nails reminds me that I matter just as much as everyone else in my family. Oh . . . and the foot and hand massages, however short, don't feel too bad either.

≈ Activate your senses. Whether you tune into your favorite station on Pandora while you're doing the dishes or you wake up your nose with the sweet smells of Kai products (you will *love* them!) during or after a long, hot shower, know that the time it takes for your little pamper session will work in your favor like a great investment.

≈ Running after the little ones or walking your dog may burn calories, but I wouldn't say they consistently take you to a happy place. They can't hurt, but the trick to endorphin production and keeping you looking and feeling your best is continuous, moderate to high-intensity exercise. It may take effort to get to the gym or to pop in a P90X video, but believe me, both your brain and your attitude, along with your reflection in the mirror, will thank you for it!

≈ If you are feeling "flat" and uninterested in things that would normally put an instant smile on your heart, talk to someone. Don't be too proud to ask for help (whether it's from a spouse, friend, mentor, counselor, or professional). Everyone needs it.

Love (and Appreciation) Will Keep Us Together

*We often take for granted the very things
that most deserve our gratitude.*

—CYNTHIA OZICK

CHAPTER THREE

ISN'T IT A SHAME THAT VALENTINE'S DAY COMES AROUND only once a year? I guess I should be grateful that it comes around at all, but as a hopeless romantic, I am sad to think that so many wait to express their affection until the grocery store stocks a couple aisles with heart-shaped boxes of chocolate and snuggly-soft teddy bears.

I'm not saying we should banish the day altogether on the grounds that it forces those in relationships to get out their credit cards and make retailers happy. As someone trying to get through life with full-force mommy brain, I need all the cues I can get to do just about anything. That includes actively appreciating my loved ones, so I welcome the reminder.

After all, what bigger responsibility do we have than letting the people we love know how much we love and appreciate them? Valentine's Day gives us a gentle nudge to take the time to do what we should do every day—not allow romance to take a backseat.

In her book *The How of Happiness*, Sonja Lyubomirsky explains that admiration and appreciation are the cornerstones of any healthy relationship. After my short nine years of marriage, I would have to agree. Expressions of gratitude and admiration, whether subtle or extravagant, are the super glue that keeps us together, helping us ride the tides of busy schedules and little frustrations, and maintain a focus on our partner, whose happiness is a part of our own. We don't always get what we want, but if our partner is there to love and support us, we can get what we need.

IN SICKNESS AND IN HEALTH, AT THE SPA AND ON THE SLOPE

Since we've been married, my thoughtful husband has traditionally sent me to a local spa for my birthday, knowing I would cherish that more than a physical gift. I get a day to feel pampered and have the cares of the world massaged away . . . at least momentarily. All I have to do is lie back and relax and say thankful prayers for being so lucky.

The other 364 days of the year, Ryan and I realize how important it is to our individual sanities to indulge in a bit of "me time," so we try our best to strike a balance of when we're each allowed to be off the parenthood clock. On the rare occasion that my girlfriends and I can plan a night away from our duties at home, I give my goodnight kisses and hand over the kids' reins to the man of the house. Pass this mama a glass of red wine and a gab session with the girls, and I'm a happy camper. On the flip side, if we wake up to a fresh-powder day in the winter, or a cool day full of sunshine in the summer, I practically shove Ryan out the door with his snowboard or mountain bike. Without that time to enjoy his passions, he would not be the man I fell in love with, and I want that man around for a really, really long time.

Part of a healthy relationship is not just creating time with each other, but creating time *for* each other. It's making sure that your partner nourishes the hobbies and passions and interests that make up the person he or she fell in love with, and vice versa. Not only is it a way of keeping resentment at a minimum, but by encouraging your partner to do what he loves, you are saying: *I love you. I appreciate you. I am grateful for you.*

There are few better feelings than those.

HAPPY LIFE, HAPPY WIFE . . . AND PARTNER

In a study published by the *Journal of Personality and Social Psychology* in 2012, Amie Gordon and her colleagues found that people who feel more appreciated by their romantic partners report being more appreciative *of* their partners.

Here's what their results revealed: When you are feeling the most grateful for your significant other, you are more committed to making your relationship last. When you are more committed to making your relationship last, you are more responsive to the needs of the one you love and become a better and more caring listener. When you are a better and more caring listener, your partner feels more appreciated by you. When your partner feels more appreciated by you, they feel more grateful *for* you—and the cycle begins again. As Gordon said, "By promoting a cycle of generosity, gratitude can actually help relationships thrive."

But not only can gratitude help those in the midst of good times get to better times, it can help those in an otherwise healthy relationship experiencing tough times breeze past them.

According to researchers at the Greater Good Science Center at the University of California, Berkeley, "When we hit a rocky patch, this research suggests, it's the upward spiral of gratitude that encourages us to risk vulnerability, tune into our partner's needs, and resolve the conflict, rather than turning away from him or her." It builds security and helps partners recognize the true value of their relationship.

To keep your relationship going strong, I suggest taking a note from my friend Erik Williams. With a marriage that is flourishing, he had this to say about the anniversary of his first date with Kim, now his wife:

> Eleven years ago today, after weeks of shameless begging, this hot young thing agreed to go on a date with me. To show her how Colorado cool I was, I took her fly-fishing for her first time. No fish . . . strike 1. She falls in and soaks the waders . . . strike 2. We go back to my apartment, where I cook her a fish dinner and burn it beyond recognition . . . strike 3.
>
> I remember that moment where everything had gone wrong: we sat at my kitchen table, and I was simply mesmerized by her. I kept thinking I was blessed among all men for being in that spot.
>
> Flash forward to last night: same girl, different table. This time there was more than charred cod between us. Three kids, two dogs, houses, cars, mortgages, jobs, grey hairs and so much life packed into those years. One of the best parts about my life is that I'm still mesmerized when I look across the table.
>
> I will love this girl every day of my life—and be grateful for the opportunity.

Based on this new research, I have a feeling that as long as Erik holds on to that gratitude, and he and Kim continue to pass it back and forth between them, the cycle of happiness will last much longer than the decade-plus they have been married. And if my son, Max, has his way, he's going to marry Bella, their sweet daughter. Erik isn't so crazy about envisioning his six-year-old walking down the aisle just yet, but if Max keeps his sights set on her, I have every confidence that in his in-laws he would have wonderful marital role models. Role models with hearts full of gratitude.

Warm Toes = A Warm Heart

Holidays are among the best times of the year to show you care. I'm definitely a fan of thoughtfully expressing your love on the days that aren't related to a holiday, but at the very least, the days of celebration in your culture should be recognized with appropriate gifts. And if you give from a place of love, odds are that the recipient will lovingly accept your gift. Remember the wise words of author Eileen Elias Freeman: "It isn't the size of the gift that matters, but the size of the heart that gives it."

When Ryan and I were first together, we were having a casual conversation about gifts. He asked me to name the worst gift I had ever received: socks. As a lifetime wearer of plain white socks, I just never saw the appeal. People usually can't see them, so why go to the effort? But in that moment, I realized that I had just cast my line out into a sea of cheesy foot coverings and would no doubt be reeling some in the next chance my future husband got.

It turned out that he got that opportunity during our first secret rendezvous arranged by the producers of *The Bachelorette*. We were holed up in a little apartment in Los Angeles and decided that since we weren't contractually allowed to be together on December 25, we would make the most of the time we were being given to exchange gifts before Santa got on his sleigh. Lo and behold, box after bag after bag after box was filled with what I had told him were my least favorite gifts, accompanied by a few hats as well. I had never appreciated them before, but Ryan changed all that—especially after I read the silly poem he wrote to go with them:

Why Socks?

Everybody loves diamonds, rings, chains of gold
But what good are diamonds when your feet get cold.
Oh no, there can only be two things for that.
A good pair of socks and a stocking hat.
One hat should do, but when it comes to socks,
They get dirty quick . . . you may need a box.
At least a drawer full. Pair upon pair.
Keep them in a drawer, next to your underwear.
I appreciate the little things, the socks of this life.
So I'll never forget the importance of my fiancée or wife.
Think of them not as a gift, but a guarantee
That I'll always love you . . . warm, soft, and wool-free.

Think about how many times you've been given a gift that couldn't have been further from your style. You say thank you, but not for what you just opened. You say it because your mama taught you proper manners and because you know that the old cliché about it being the thought that counts was spot on.

That Christmas I didn't really want or need a drawer full of comical and cozy socks. Every time I unwrapped another pair, though, my laughter became more genuine and my heart more full. He had managed to show me that it was truly the little things that could make me feel the most love. And to this day, the little things are what I cherish the most.

A BLESSED BROKEN ROAD

When I first heard the song "Bless the Broken Road" by Rascal Flatts, it was instantly one of my all-time favorites. If you've heard neither their version nor the original recording by Nitty Gritty Dirt Band, head to iTunes and take a listen. It's a poignant song about how all relationships, especially the ones that shatter our hearts into teeny-tiny pieces, lead us to the one we are ultimately meant to find.

Every time I hear it, I can't help but feel it was written for me, and I'm positive that I'm not alone. Many of us can relate to it, and for good reason. Like millions of other fans, I've had my share of eye-opening heartbreak on the path to finding the love of my life.

It all started in high school with the first boy I ever loved. I met him in the seventh grade and we became a pair the next year. He was the life of any party, with all-American good looks, a charming personality, a loving mother, a bright future on the football field, and friends in every corner of the school. For about five years, we rode the roller coaster of a high school relationship, going from boyfriend/girlfriend, to boy-interested-in-other-girls/girl-still-infatuated-with-boy-and-acting-like-she's-not, back to boyfriend/girlfriend, then to just friends, and so on and so on. No matter our status, I wanted to be with him.

My diaries from that time period are filled with hearts and smiley faces, even when he either intentionally or unintentionally hurt me. I was so blinded by puppy love that I couldn't see the bottom line: he wasn't as in love with me as I was with him. It didn't matter if he had moved on to a girl from a rival high school, or was dating one of my close friends. If he gave me even a morsel of sweet attention, I clung to it, and I'm pretty sure he knew I would.

For most of those five years, I allowed my boyfriend/friend/subject of infatuation to motivate my decisions and most of my happiness, and as it tends to do if we aren't paying close enough attention, history repeated itself. This time it was with a guy I met during my second year of graduate school. He was new to the University of Miami physical therapy program, and I was new to the single world after ending a two-year relationship. We hit it off and stayed together for nearly two years, but a string of straws in the form of tangible evidence that he was less than faithful broke this camel's back.

One straw was a handwritten letter from one of his lady "friends" who had been visiting while I was away, saying "be good, or at least be good until we can be bad together." Other straws included pictures I found of him on spring break dancing in a not-so-innocent way with a girl I had never seen before, and a chain of e-mail messages that discussed what he and his best friend jokingly called "orgy at the Colony." The Colony was the apartment complex where we lived together, and the weekend they were discussing inviting over a bevy of beauties was one that I had invited him to a wedding and he'd declined, saying his sister would be visiting. Yep, he played the family card, and yep, I bought it.

I continued to deny my instincts and trust that the love I felt for him was mutual. But his actions repeatedly showed me that I wasn't a priority in his life, and he wasn't ready to commit. I just didn't want to see it. I didn't want to lose him. I didn't want to be alone.

Over and over again, for years and years, I sacrificed my psychological well-being just to be in a relationship. I blindly loved both of these men to the detriment of my own personal happiness. I deserved more. We all deserve more.

I wish I could spare my younger self the repeated smashing of all the eggs I put in those baskets, but I've settled on taking the lessons I learned from them (and the rest of my failed relationships) and using them to be the best wife I can be. Without those failures, I wouldn't have found relationship success. No experience, no matter how bad, is a waste—unless you waste the lesson. It took a few lessons, but in the end, I couldn't be more grateful that my broken road led me straight to Ryan and my happy ending.

Modern Family

For more and more couples these days, divorce ends up being the only option left in creating a future with hope and happiness—my parents included. Whatever the reason, some couples decide that their lives would be better without the person they once said they wanted to dedicate the rest of forever to. And for some, it's the wise choice.

Having lived a short forty years, I can count on one hand how many of my friends have decided to end their marital relationships. One of these is a friend from college I became close with through Redsteppers, otherwise known as the dancers who performed with the band during halftime at Indiana University football games in bright red knee-high leather boots. I had lost touch with her for a few years after we both graduated, but now I see her beautiful face on *E! News*. To me, she was Cathy Sadler. To America, she's known as Catt.

I knew that Catt went through a divorce and had recently met her new Prince Charming, but I didn't know the full story until she posted an article she wrote for *Genlux* magazine. The second I finished reading it, I sent her a text asking if I could share it with you here, thinking that if divorce is the only option after all others have been considered, then Catt and her extended family are an excellent example of how to gratefully move forward in the shadow of sadness. She gladly agreed to let me share an excerpt. Happy reading (and THANK YOU, Catt!):

A Joy Division

I never thought I'd get divorced. I was a child of divorce and to me the D word was a dirty one.

I was just entering my thirties, my two children were growing and thriving, my career was advancing, but my marriage to Kyle was crumbling. We were college sweethearts, solid friends, and managing our full lives together side by side. But, as the old cliché goes, we were growing apart. After more than twelve years together, eight of them married, our relationship began to dissolve.

But the details of our decline aren't as important as what came after.

In 2007, I woke up a single mom of two living thousands of miles away from my family back home in Indiana. But I couldn't lay in bed self-loathing, I had to soldier on for my boys. Thankfully, I had a fantastic TV job in Los Angeles hosting a show that challenged me creatively and also filled me emotionally. The *Daily 10* cast and crew were like family. My job brought laughter into my life every day and was in many ways an escape from the heartache I was feeling after my divorce.

Time passed, and eventually I began to understand that for Kyle and me, being friends was better than being husband and wife; and I also felt that our children were adjusting well, all things considered.

When my older son Austin turned seven, I hosted a birthday party at our home. Several of the kids' friends were invited, my girlfriends and their husbands were there, and, of course, Kyle wouldn't miss it. I knew he had been dating Sarah for several months, so when he respectfully called beforehand to ask if she could come to the party, I said yes.

My friends were astonished. "How are you corralling kids, overseeing the face painting, leading the happy birthday song, and not losing your mind knowing 'she' is here?"

And then something happened. Sarah asked if I could use her help.

A moment later I was cutting the cake and Sarah was scooping the ice cream. We were side by side. It was then and there, in that very moment, I knew it wasn't about me. It wasn't about us. It was about the boys. It was about forgiveness. And most of all, it was about love.

Fast forward more than four years and Sarah and Kyle are married. I, too, have found love again. I married Rhys last October. And today, long after divorce, I consider my family to be progressive, healthy, and according to many who know us, even inspirational.

Our Modern Family exists because of a conscious choice to put our children first. Once that determination was made, the fruits of that decision included a continued friendship post-marriage with my ex, and eventually new friendships between all four of the adults involved. Sarah and Rhys not only support and encourage the "Joy Division" as we know it today, but they are an integral part of it.

I genuinely want to alert others to the possibilities of what life can be like after divorce. It is possible to reboot and achieve a symbiotic, thriving family dynamic. Sure, if one person in the group had not had the same vision, none of this would be possible. But ours is love—divided, and conquered.

Speak Now or Forever Hold Your Peace

I know many people hate them, but I love surprises. My husband knows this about me and has a way of pulling off a surprise without my having the faintest idea that something special is headed my way. I guess that's what a surprise is all about.

On our first anniversary, we were offered the opportunity to shoot a show called *Trista and Ryan's Honeymoon Hotspots* for the Travel Channel. Due to our business schedules, we weren't able to travel to all ten international destinations on the list, but we weren't complaining when we got the green light to head to our first choice: South Africa. Not only were we able to arrange a dream vacation to a place neither of us had ever been, but we scheduled it around our first wedding anniversary so we could celebrate it in an extra-special way.

The trip was nothing short of spectacular (including a little surprise I arranged to have a local African minister renew our vows), but what I remember most about it was a note I received a couple weeks after we got home. I could describe it to you, but after correcting a bit of fading, I thought it would be more fun to show you:

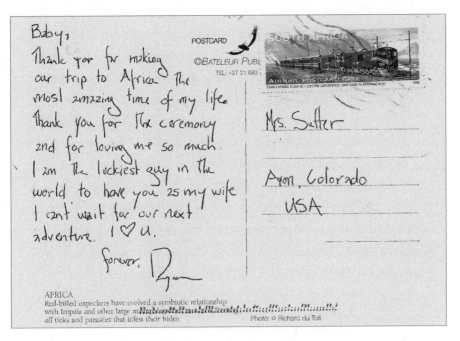

My hubby had purchased, written, and sent a postcard to me during our trip without tipping me off. So that I never forget the ultra-sweet gesture, I keep the card right at eye level in front of my desk. The writing is faded and the stamp is torn, but the sentiment will never get old.

According to a study by Dr. Terri Orbuch, author of *5 Simple Steps to Take Your Marriage from Good to Great,* the happiest couples are those who often say thank you to each other. In an article for the *Huffington Post*, Orbuch wrote that 61 percent of the couples she studied "said that their spouses 'often' made them feel good about the kind of person they are." The gratitude she studied came from "words, gestures or acts" that let partners know that they were "noticed, appreciated, respected, loved or desired." She didn't mention exorbitant purchases or fantastical adventures. She mentioned words, kindnesses, and small gestures—the little things of this life (such as a poem about socks or even the socks themselves).

I'll never forget the day Ryan was at work and I found a sweet surprise on the shower wall. He had used the letters the kids play with in the bath to spell out "ILU"—our abbreviation for "I love you." The rest of the day, I couldn't stop smiling.

So sweet. So simple. So incredibly special.

Another wonderful gesture came on our copper anniversary, aka anniversary number seven. He called his poem "A Pound of Pennies for My Thoughts" and included an actual pound of shiny new pennies from the US Mint. I've edited his poem a touch, because there are a few parts I'd like to keep private (if you catch my drift), but here are the meat and potatoes:

A Pound of Pennies for My Thoughts

A pound of pennies,
One for each thought
Or each reason or each cause
Or each lesson you've taught
Or each moment I've realized
How much I love you.
How much I love you because of . . .

Your smile
Your love
The way you care so much
The way you love your kids

Love (and Appreciation) Will Keep Us Together

The way you love me

Your toes

How you look in jeans

That you let me be me

Your forgiveness

That you only buy white cars

You moved to the mountains

You want to stay in the mountains

Your charity

Your loyalty

You hate my black socks

Your thoughtful gifts

You in a pony tail

You're ticklish

How you make pumpkin pie

You never miss a "favorite part of the day"

When I'm your "favorite part of the day"

How the kids love you

That I'll always love you

That you'll always love me

You are a good friend

You are a great friend

You are my best friend

That you're my wife

That we've been married 7 years

That we'll be married 7 more, and 7 more . . .

That this list was really easy

That your last name is Sutter

That I love you more . . .

Have you shown your partner you appreciate him or her lately? Whether it's through a hug, a note, or even a simple thank-you, tell your partner while you have the chance. As the great French novelist Marcel Proust said, "Let's be grateful for those who give us happiness; they are the charming gardeners who make our soul bloom."

You never know what tomorrow will bring, but you certainly have the power to share the happiness you feel today. I've even included a list of suggestions so you can't use the excuse that you couldn't think of anything!

- ✣ Send them flowers or a cool bamboo plant at work with a note that says "I miss you."

- ✣ On a starry night, put the kids to bed, break open a bottle of your favorite "poison," lay down side by side on a cozy blanket, and watch for shooting stars. Make wishes for each other and your future.

- ✣ Carve your initials on a tree that stands in a spot your partner won't be able to miss—maybe it's on a favorite hiking trail, or maybe it's in your front yard. Just make sure it's at eye level.

HAPPILY EVER ACTIONS

〰 Just as Ryan did for me, create a list for your partner of the many reasons you love him or her. Start it with "I love you because . . . " and let the words flow onto the paper. Believe me, your partner will appreciate every single one.

≈ Schedule date nights. I married my husband because he's my favorite person on earth. What's better than giving back to myself (and hopefully to him) by sharing a night with the person I chose to share my life with?

≈ If date night is a good idea, then date weekend is even better, right? Plan a getaway to a nearby town, or even a weekend stay at a local hotel. Go visit friends, see the sights of a town you've always had on your bucket list, or just get a change of scenery. The resultant positive change in your relationship will be worth it.

≈ Stockpile greeting cards. Go through your stash on a day that is in threat of never being remembered or one that will be remembered for all bad reasons. After writing sweet nothings in the card, put it in a spot your honey won't be able to miss. Think computer screen or bathroom sink or refrigerator. You may just turn that day into one of the best ever.

≈ There's no time like the present to learn from the lessons of the past. Think of the significant relationships from your life and list five things you learned from them to better yourself from here on out. Understanding the reason for an ending can give you a greater vision of how to create new beginnings and better forevers.

Tiny Humans
with Big Hearts

Never fear spoiling children by making them too happy. Happiness is the atmosphere in which all good affections grow.

—THOMAS BRAY

CHAPTER FOUR

AS A YOUNG GIRL, I PRAYED THAT GOD WOULD BLESS me with the gift of becoming a mother one day. I dreamed about the joys of motherhood and experiencing the unconditional love I knew I would have for my own flesh and blood. Later in life, when I learned I was pregnant and those prayers would soon be answered, I started saying new prayers. First and foremost was for God to bless me with a healthy child. Next on the long list of hopes for my baby were the qualities of respect, happiness, curiosity, creativity, humor, faith, intelligence, courage, kindness, confidence, and last but certainly not least . . . gratitude.

I realize that it is my job as a parent to provide a good example, but I definitely have bad days where I lose my cool after stepping in the "presents" that our Yorkie leaves on the carpet, get in an awful argument with my husband, or, even worse, learn that my eighty-nine-year-old grandmother, Rose, has been admitted to the hospital again. As much as I want to stay down in the dumps in those moments, for the sake of my family, I change my socks, wipe away my tears, and try not to dwell on them. I want my kids to do the same.

When Max and Blakesley were each about two years old, we started a bedtime routine of saying prayers. Every night, the prayers start out the same: "Thank you for today." As the German philosopher Meister Eckhart once said, "If the only prayer you ever say in your entire life is thank you, it will be enough." I personally have a strong belief that God has a plan for us, and we should recognize the incredible blessing we've been given of experiencing another day on earth—good, bad, or indifferent. As a parent, I will encourage my kids to make their own decisions when it comes to their religious beliefs, but I truly hope, whatever they end up believing, that they embrace the idea of expressing gratitude to a higher power through a daily acknowledgment of thanks.

I realize that four- and six-year-olds can't properly grasp the idea of a grand scheme of the universe. I do hope that by placing nuggets of optimism in their minds, though, that at the very least they will be more likely to have sweet dreams.

Happy thoughts beget a happy existence. Even in moments of sorrow and grief, gratitude brings positive thoughts to the forefront of your consciousness.

I have many goals as a parent, but my highest priority is doing everything I can to ensure that my kids' worlds are bursting with joy. Sometimes I do it by making silly faces or dancing like I have ants in my pants, but if I go one step further and help them find a way to be grateful for anything that gives them a glimmer of a smile, I know I have truly succeeded.

FINDING YOUR SAFE, HAPPY PLACE IN A CRUEL, CRUEL WORLD

I will never forget what Ryan's elderly grandmother, Norane, said to her great-grandson when she first met him. As she cradled our tiny baby in her arms, she said, "Maxwell, it's a cruel, cruel world." As a doting new mother, I instantly feared that her gloomy words would find their way into my son's spirit and cause a wound that would fester from the inside out (as I may have mentioned, I have a tendency to be a dramatic worrywart). As a realist, though, I knew that no matter how much I worked to protect my family from the iniquities around us, she was right.

As time has gone on, I've found that on a pretty regular basis I have to comfort my tiny tots for any number of hurts small and large (of course, I am more than happy to oblige). It may be on the second day of one of Ryan's forty-eight-hour shifts, and they start to miss their daddy. It could be when they are lethargic and blowing snot bubbles thanks to the latest virus that has invaded our community, or when their feelings are hurt because things didn't go their way on the playground. The possibilities are endless—just like the almost nightly reassurances that Blakesley required around the age of three.

Without fail, just as I would go to close the door and blow her goodnight kisses, she would tearily say, "Mommy, I don't want it to rain and funder." For most adults, thunderstorms can be calming, or at least negligible, unless of course they are watching one out of the window of an airplane (been there, done that, and I do not recommend it). For my daughter, one especially loud night when she was almost three years old developed into a fear that we were unable to resolve for about six months. At first, I thought she was using it as a stall tactic, conjuring up anything she could to put off falling asleep for a few minutes more. However, when the tears started flowing, I realized that she was either genuinely frightened or an extremely talented actress.

Either way, she clearly needed more mommy time. I always gently reminded her that even if it rains and "funders," she is safe and sound in a warm and cozy bed with a roof over her head and a house full of love.

I felt those moments were perfect opportunities to change negatives to positives and build the ideas of trust and safety inside her head, and I do the same for Max when the occasion arises. I know the ideas alone can't keep my precious children out of harm's way, but it's definitely a start—an important foundation to lay down before they are able to understand the news reports and the live discussions about the tragedies of the world that they may overhear. Tragedies, such as those in Westminster, Colorado, and Newtown, Connecticut, that don't involve anyone we personally know, but that have been incredibly persuasive in compelling me to put on a positively focused parenting hat.

The first rocked our nation on October 10, 2012, when authorities found the body of ten-year-old Jessica Ridgeway. Five days earlier, Jessica had left her house to meet friends at a nearby park to walk to school together. She never made it. Somewhere along the short walk between her home and the park, a predator plucked her off the street. I can only assume from the news reports that what happened afterward was heinous.

Until this unspeakable crime happened just hours from our home, I'd always considered the mountains to be somewhat sheltered from the ugliness of the world. There are, of course, unlawful things that happen in the Vail Valley, but compared to the gruesome murders and abductions in the big cities I have lived in, they always seemed so trivial.

Not anymore.

That's even more true after the second tragedy in Newtown. On December 14, 2012, this town, described in reports as quiet and scenic, was terrorized by a disturbed twenty-year-old. Within five minutes of arriving at Sandy Hook Elementary School that day, he had unloaded 154 rounds of ammunition with an assault rifle and caused a lifetime of irreparable psychological damage to the survivors, as well as their families and friends, the larger community, and even to our nation as a whole. He took not only the lives of twenty innocent six- and seven-year-olds, but those of six heroic adults, most of whom dedicated their final moments to protecting the children within their reach.

The Newtown gunman made that school his target of terror, and just as Jessica Ridgeway's predator made us question the safety of a short walk to the park, he tainted the sanctity of schools around the country. For a person with the heart of a mother, these barbaric deaths immediately stirred up deep sadness, worry, and anger. Just the thought of anything remotely like that happening to Max or Blakesley made me want to take up residence in a barricaded fortress and never leave.

But I realize that giving in to the fear would be giving in to the bad guys. To keep my head in the game of life, I had to keep moving forward and not allow the weight of others' evil actions to take me down . . . at least not all the way. Sorrow and fear can be overwhelming, but as parents we have to stay strong and brave for the pint-size people who continue to look up to us for guidance. More than ever, we need to ask how we can help ensure the safety of our most precious gifts—our babies.

Since we can't always guarantee the security of our surroundings or be with our school-age children every minute of every day, our job is to shape their impressionable minds through a balancing act between acknowledging the existence of darkness so they can do their best to keep themselves safe, and helping them focus on the far more prevalent light and love of the world. As Fred "Mister" Rogers once said, "When I was a boy and I would see scary things in the news, my mother would say to me, 'Look for the helpers. You will always find people who are helping.' To this day, especially in times of 'disaster,' I remember my mother's words, and I am always comforted by realizing that there are still so many helpers—so many caring people in this world."

Yes, tragedy brings families and friends and communities together, but I would rather live in peaceful naïveté than lose a young angel to heaven too soon. My hope, like all caring parents around the world, is to keep my angels around as long as possible, to shelter them from pain, and to give them a life happier than my own. The world may fall short at protecting them, but I will always remain steadfast in my love for them and my determination to not end my years telling my great-grandchildren what a "cruel, cruel world" it is.

I believe in the beauty of the human spirit and I want my kids to as well.

An Aptitude for Gratitude

When Max was three years old, Ryan explained to him that he couldn't go to ski school because he was sick. Max replied, "Yeah, but I'm happy!" In his mind, it didn't matter if he could spread viral germs all over the mountain, including to his ski buddies and instructor. It mattered that he had awakened on the right side of the bed and *really* wanted to go. That's the mentality of a preschooler: innocent egotism.

As children grow older, biological egotism doesn't need to continue into developed egotism. Yes, confidence is healthy, but a confident kid without altruistic tendencies can turn into an ungrateful and selfish adult. No parent I know wants that. Parents want to do everything in their power to put their children on a path to generosity and goodwill, and as a recent study showed, they can, even with babies as young as fifteen months old.

In an effort to examine whether twelve- to fifteen-month-olds had yet developed an understanding of fairness, Jessica Sommerville, an early childhood development expert and University of Washington researcher, observed whether they shared toys selfishly or unselfishly. What Sommerville found was that in the participating infants, there was a close alliance between sharing and expectations of what was fair. The children who were sensitive to inequalities were able to share in an altruistic way. More important, though, Sommerville concluded that the behaviors stemming from comprehending fairness likely are learned at a much earlier age than previously thought.

If we can start to teach our children how to be fair and caring in the second year of life, I would surmise that we can also begin to teach them how to appreciate being cared for or being shown kindness, as well. And there is no better way to get into the gears of mini minds than by personal involvement. As Benjamin Franklin said, "Tell me and I forget. Teach me and I remember. Involve me and I learn."

I take that idea to heart.

HAPPILY EVER AFTER

After a tragic local event, I was spurred to help members of our community while involving Max and Blakesley (then four and three years old) in what I felt could be a valuable lesson in altruism and caring. It was an especially windy and dry day during a season of wildland fires that had destroyed hundreds of thousands of acres of land. I was sitting in a parking lot trying to calm myself down after an argument with Ryan (yes, we do argue, and no, it isn't important what we were arguing about) when I heard the rare sound of emergency vehicle sirens. Curiosity got the best of me, so I drove in the direction of the crowds and commotion and ended up parking with dozens of other cars across the highway from the largest blaze I had ever seen in person. It had engulfed a four-unit condominium complex and was gaining power thanks to excessive wind and the drought that had overtaken our tiny valley.

After hours of working hard, firefighters (including Ryan, who was on duty that day) contained the flames. What was left: blackened rubble (thankfully, no one had been seriously injured). The residents of these homes that we drove past every day had lost everything, and it broke my heart. To this day, whenever we drive past, the kids, without fail, comment on "the broken house." After hearing that one of the families had a little person, just like them, and another on the way, I knew my children would join me in doing what we could to get them and the other victims back on their feet.

I spent weeks sending e-mails back and forth to companies I had worked with, asking them to send anything from clothing to shoes, diapers to baby bedding, toiletries to toys. Even in our tough economy, most of them came through. I was thrilled!

At home, the kids and I gathered items we knew the little girl would love, including Max's old Bratt Decor crib. We talked about how lucky we were to have a home and a bed, shampoo and Band-Aids, sweatshirts and sneakers, and lots and lots of toys that we could now share with a family who had lost all of theirs.

We scheduled a day to bring boxes of what we had gathered to a local church where the mother of the little girl worked. The woman got her daughter out of child care, and I had Blakesley hand her a headband and bow that she had picked out herself. Meanwhile, Max sorted through the supplies and brought our attention to everything he found to be interesting (which, at four years old, was just about anything). Blakesley's new little friend wasn't as taken by hair bows as my older girly-girl, but that didn't take away from the joy of giving that Blakesley experienced.

For the rest of the day, we talked about what Max and Blakesley had done, especially when we drove by the burnt remnants of the condo complex. I reinforced how that family was just like us but a bad accident had left them without many of the things we are blessed to have at home. By bringing those supplies to our new friends and openly discussing their situation, I was hoping to teach my kiddos a bit about the art of giving as well as the concept of gratitude, and I think it worked.

Six months later, I knew it had . . . at least for Max.

One night in November 2012 as I was getting in the Thanksgiving spirit, I pulled Max's covers up and asked him what he was grateful for. His answer: "My bed, because not everyone has one."

My heart smiled.

Throughout my kids' childhood, my husband and I plan to continue to teach them any chance we get. It needn't be after the devastation of a fire, of course. Hopefully that will never happen to anyone we know again. On any day of the year, they can learn to be grateful for something as minor as their daddy taking the time to put batteries back in their favorite toy, or as major as getting an extra-long hug from Mickey Mouse himself.

So, do your little ones a favor: don't assume that a grateful and gracious person is born that way. The job of a parent or caregiver is even more important than providing a safe, warm, happy place for children to grow (and we all know that can be difficult enough at times). Not only should you strive to give them the basics of survival, but you should also make it a priority to teach them the art of appreciation and gratitude. Both their lives and all of our futures will be set on a more hopeful course to happiness.

KIDS ARE GRATEFUL FOR THE DARNEDEST (AND MOST PROFOUND) THINGS

Just like the kids who appeared on the television shows that aired in the 1950s and late '90s, my children tell it like it is. That holds true for the things they say about gratitude.

To (shamelessly) show how insanely adorable my kids and their friends and my friends' kids are, I wanted to share what some of their responses were to the question: "What are you grateful for?"

It doesn't get much cuter than this:

- Maxwell (Sutter), age four: "I am thankful for my family and Batman. They help me."

- Reese, age six: "I'm grateful for my brother because he gives me someone to look up to. I'm also grateful for sparkles in nail polish."
- Will, age eight: "I'm grateful for my life and my family . . . and my Xbox360. I'm also grateful that I know how to read and write because it is a very good skill to know. It's gonna make me rich one day."
- Jules, age three: "I am thankful for my friend Sophie 'cause I love her and we eat lollipops at dance class."
- Brielle, age seven: "I'm grateful that I have my family, nature, and my freedom."
- Estela, age four: "I'm grateful for my family, for my brother, for my dog Toulouse, for my beautiful house and room, for going to Disney, for going to gymnastics, my beautiful friends, for Jesus and the angels, my *abuelos* and Gran-mama and Pop, and everything I have, my cousins, all my toys, that my mommy had me, that Papa is a king and Mama a queen. . . . " (In the interest of time, her mommy, Ali Landry, pushed the pause button. Seems like she's on a great course to writing a book on gratitude herself one day!)
- Berkley, age three: "I'm grateful for Mommy and Daddy, Sleeping Beauty, Snow White, and everything."
- Jax, age four: "I'm thankful for the trees because they give lots of fruit to people who need food and Spider-Man because he protects us."

EDUCATION AT ITS BEST

In early 2012, I was contacted by Stephanie Rea, a teacher who follows me on Twitter. She wanted to know my thoughts on using the "favorite part of the day" activity in her classroom. She got the idea from my nightly posts and decided the activity could be beneficial for her students. I couldn't have been more excited! The school setting seemed like the perfect place for a daily reflection of gratitude.

I found out later that not only had Stephanie gotten her students to bring a great part of the day to the forefront of their thoughts, but she implemented use of a "My Blessings" book where they kept a log of each day's happy memory.

After starting her class's gratitude program, she wrote me to say, "Thank you for the idea. It's amazing how taking one minute out of a busy day to reflect can change your view on life! You are inspirational and my students are thankful for this!"

Right back at ya, Stephanie. Thank you for recognizing the possibility for change and having such a special impact on the children in your community. Keep up the *great* work!

GENERATIONS OF GRATITUDE

No matter your title at work—president, manager, executive assistant—if you are a parent, caring for your children is the most important job you have, or it should be. Most likely, it's also the most selfless job you have. Certainly one without monetary compensation and probably without even simple thanks, especially if you are the parent of an infant or teenager. You may not hear voluntary expressions of gratitude come out of their little (or *big*) mouths every day, but the rewards run so much deeper, and you can take them with you for years and years to come.

Knowing how wonderful it feels to have my kids say "I love you, Mommy" without prompting makes me question how often I gave my own parents those special rewards of acknowledgment when I was a child. I realize now that it wasn't nearly as frequently as I should have. I obviously can't change the past. What I can do is honor my parents' legacy.

Before our kids were born, Ryan and I decided that one of the most profound ways to do that was through the names we chose for their grandchildren. Our firstborn, Maxwell Alston Sutter, shares his middle name with "Grampa B" (Ryan's dad), and our baby girl was given my mother's maiden name: Blakesley. Upon hearing the news about her namesake, my mother sent me this note: "This is the most incredible 'gratitude gift' I could ever receive," she wrote. "It says 'thank you for all you did when I was growing up,' it says 'thank you to Grandma and Grandpa for being who they are.' It says, 'I'm proud of my family.' It is a gift that will always be remembered! Love you, Mama!"

I hope that every time my children hear their names, a little happy spark inside them reminds them of the legacy of their family, a legacy to be proud of.

TRADITIONAL THANKS

Every year, on the fourth Thursday of November, Americans gather around dining room tables or card tables or anywhere they can find a spot, and feast in honor of a day that originally celebrated a successful harvest. A national Thanksgiving Day holiday was the brainchild of Sarah Josepha Hale, an influential American writer and editor who lobbied five US presidents to officially observe a day that, for years, only New England celebrated. After reading her letter, President Abraham Lincoln agreed, deciding our country needed a little positive focus during the struggles of the Civil War. Smart woman—and man.

Besides the annual trip from St. Louis to Evansville, Indiana, and devouring my grandmother's homemade mashed potatoes and candied yams, my family never really established any traditions of giving thanks. As the mother of our family's next generation, that's one thing I decided to change. My friend Evin gave me the perfect idea of how to do that.

Every year she can remember, and probably even before that, the Thanksgiving celebration in Evin's family has started exactly the same way. When the turkey and fixin's are about ready, the family gathers around the dining room table, which is rich in history and memories—it has been around since 1920 and was once owned by her great-grandparents. Everyone holds hands. After saying grace, Evin's father, Tom Garretson, asks for a moment of silence: "Let's remember those who have stood here before us and those who can't be with us." He then proceeds to squeeze the hand of the person to his right, who then squeezes the hand of the person to his or her right, and so on, until those squeezes wrap around the entire table, connecting everyone with a simple gesture of love. Then, from youngest to oldest, each person reveals one thing he or she is grateful for. It's a tradition that fills their hearts and souls in a much more lasting way than even the most delicious turkey, stuffing, cranberry sauce, and pumpkin pie can do.

We may not have an antique table to circle around in our home, but I am committed to making sure that all the other pieces of their gratitude puzzle find a place with us this Thanksgiving and every year thereafter. Thanks, Evin!

FOLLOW MY LEAD

American writer Clarence Budington Kelland once said something that really resonates with me, something I think about every day: "He didn't tell me how to live; he lived, and let me watch him do it."

Nothing proves the veracity of this sentiment like living with a preschooler. If I raise my voice at our anxiety-ridden Yorkie, Tank—who barks so intensely when we leave the house that our neighborhood must think we should be reported to PETA—I know that my kids will start mimicking me, pleading with the dog to take it down a notch or twelve as my voice rises a notch or twelve.

The same goes for the flip side. When I catch Blakesley rocking her doll, Baby Mia, to sleep, saying, "It's okay, baby," and reading her stories, my heart swells with the knowledge that the countless hours I've done the same with her on my lap have made an impression.

We look to the elders in our life—friends, teachers, aunts and uncles, and those we have to thank for our very existence—to show us how it's done, especially when we're young.

Through a friend, I learned of a graduation speech for the University of Pennsylvania's class of 2012, which was published on the website Daily Good. It was given by Nipun Mehta, founder of ServiceSpace.org. As the ending to his speech that May, he shared a story with the graduates about his great-grandfather that I found particularly touching and relevant. I didn't have the chance to get to know my great-grandparents, but if I had, I'd have wanted them to be just like this man.

I want to close with a story about my great-grandfather. He was a man of little wealth who still managed to give every single day of his life. Each morning, he had a ritual of going on a walk—and as he walked, he diligently fed the anthills along his path with small pinches of wheat flour. Now that is an act of micro generosity so small that it might seem utterly negligible, in the grand scheme of the universe. How does it matter? It matters in that it changed him inside. And my great-grandfather's goodness shaped the worldview of my grandparents who in turn influenced that of their children— my parents. Today those ants and the anthills are gone, but my great-grandpa's spirit is very much embedded in all my actions and their future ripples. It is precisely these small, often invisible, acts of inner transformation that mold the stuff of our being, and bend the arc of our shared destiny.

On your walk, today and always, I wish you the eyes to see the anthills and the heart to feed them with joy.

May you be blessed. Change yourself—change the world.

HAPPILY EVER ACTIONS

My sorority sister Casley told me of a sweet nightly activity she does with her son Sam. As she tucks him in and turns on his nightlight, filling the ceiling with stars, they each choose one, make a wish, and say something they are thankful for. If you don't have a similar nightlight, improvise with the stars outside or even something like eyelashes or belly buttons. It's not only a way to remind yourself of your blessings, but also to create a bond with your child that will continue long past their brief childhood.

≈ At our friend Joel Dekanich's fortieth birthday party, his kids read forty reasons they are grateful for their dad. What a special way to celebrate! This can be used for anything—birthdays, holidays, anniversaries, or just as a thank-you-for-being-you moment.

≈ Take a lesson from the book of childhood and touch base with your inner preschooler every once in a while. Embrace the simple joys of life as if you were still seeing it through innocent eyes, just as Phoebe demonstrated to Rachel on an episode of *Friends* when she showed her how much more fun running through Central Park was if you wildly flailed your arms. I also highly recommend skipping! If you don't want to look quite so silly, you can also belt out "The Wheels on the Bus" in the comfort of your own home or reenact Cameron Diaz's famous booty shake in *Charlie's Angels*. I dare you to let loose and get giggling.

≈ Helping my kids lay the foundation for self-confidence is one of the biggest honors of my life. To help them believe in their own inner beauty, I try to provide a good example of healthy self-esteem, I offer positive reinforcement whenever humanly possible, and I have them repeat their "magic words" every night (inspired by the movie *The Help*). The phrases are slightly different based on the kids' individual personalities, but both start with the same statement: "I am kind." To do the same, choose a word or string of words that will help encourage your child's sense of self-worth and remember what Geoffrey Canada, an American activist and educator, once said: "You want kids really thinking 'I'm somebody special.' Have them say that every day and they grow up believing it."

⮩ Create an environment of empathy by expecting your kids to complete certain age-appropriate chores, such as feeding your family pet, making their beds, or tidying up their toys. As Charlotte Latvala described on Parents.com, by participating in daily work duties, children will gain a much stronger understanding of the effort that goes into the everyday and appreciate your hard work that much more.

⮩ Take a hint from NothingButCountry.com and have your kids or family create an Appreciation Jar. It could be for a teacher or camp counselor, a grandparent or family friend. Maybe it's for a special day, or maybe just a little pick-me-up. Regardless, it's simple: cut out hearts from construction paper and have pertinent people write something they appreciate about the recipient. Decorate the jar together, as you'd like, and make sure to take in all the joy that will undoubtedly resonate from that special person in your little one's life.

All in the Extended Family

Other things may change us,
but we start and end with family.

—ANTHONY BRANDT

CHAPTER FIVE

M Y LIFE ON EARTH STARTED AT 12:46 P.M. ON October 28, 1972. It was a day of significance commemorated only by an official hospital photo and the sweet words my mother recorded in a baby book: "Father was allowed to be in the delivery room and the labor room, and he loved every minute." I'm not sure that my mom felt the same as my dad until the pain of childbirth was over, but as far as I'm concerned, from the moment I cried my first cry, I can't remember a time that I didn't feel loved.

Since my childhood, whether I deserved it or not, my parents have been my faithful fans. And the same holds true for the support I've received from the rest of my family, both immediate and extended—including the thoughtful woman my father married after my parents' divorce; the Sewings, who caringly took me in as an honorary family member so that I wouldn't be alone while my mom went to work; and even those I didn't see that often, such as my grandparents, aunts, uncles, and cousins. Reality television then led me to Ryan and a whole new set of family members who, despite the circuslike intrusion of pop culture chaos that we brought to their lives, have always made me feel welcome and cherished.

My blended extended family is full of different personalities, lifestyles, hardships, careers, interests, hopes, and dreams, and thanks to that diversity and history, I have been taught important lessons about how to live a (mostly) happy life. They may not have been written down or verbally explained during a formal course, but through their example and willingness to share their stories, every member of my extended family has shown me a unique way to approach life.

Everyone has access to these lessons. Whether from your grandfather's ninety years of experience, your four-year-old cousin's enlightening viewpoint on the beauty of nature, or merely from the conversations you have with those who share your last name, our relatives are a seminar on life available to each of us should we simply choose to show up for class. You may not live in the same house or even the same country as they do, but when you were born, you were biologically linked to them, with their connective threads of yarn inescapably woven into your own personal tapestry.

Life is short. Neither you nor your relatives is going to be around forever. Take advantage of the remarkable gift of family and connect with them while you still can. The distinct knowledge, experiences, and outlooks they possess will expand your horizons and illuminate an understanding of another time or place, helping to shape your own path to a fortunate future.

GETTING TO KNOW YOU

Thanks to the birds and the bees, or maybe even science, your family tree added a teeny-tiny branch on the day you were born. Stemming from two separate limbs that came together as one, you became part of the big picture of your heritage, full of history and culture, events and relationships.

For me, I was always thankful for the past that led to my present, but it wasn't necessarily something I was keenly interested in. After losing my grandmoth`er, Ruth Rehn, on March 4, 2013, though, I started feeling the urge to learn more, not only as a way to keep her memory alive, but also as a way to show my children an important part of where they came from. Interestingly enough, soon after she passed away, I came across a *New York Times* article that discussed something called the "Do You Know Scale" (DYK) and the results of a study showing that it was "the best single predictor of children's emotional health and happiness."

After Dr. Robyn Fivush realized that the learning-disabled students she worked with who knew more about their families were better able to face challenges, she joined forces with Dr. Marshall Duke and developed the DYK. The test gathers answers about family history that the children could not have personally experienced, including questions such as: "Do you know where your grandparents met?"; "Do you know the names of the schools your mom went to?"; and "Do you know the source of your name?"

In 2001 Duke and Fivush posed the DYK to four dozen families and found that "higher scores on the Do You Know Scale were associated with higher levels of self-esteem, an internal locus of control (a belief in one's own capacity to control what happens to him or her), better family functioning, lower levels of anxiety, fewer behavioral problems, and better chances for good outcomes if a child faces educational or emotional/behavioral difficulties."

With further research, however, they were able to determine that it wasn't solely the act of learning facts about their families that positively influenced these children—it was the way in which they gained this knowledge and what developed as a result.

Let me explain.

Depending on the dynamics and personalities of family members, the narratives within the group can be one of three types. Either they are ascending (e.g., "we came from nothing, and with hard work we are now blessed"), descending (e.g., "we were blessed and now we have nothing"), or oscillating (e.g., "we've had ups and downs, but through it all, we had each other and will always be blessed"). Unlike the other types, the adolescents who experience oscillating narratives are not only knowledgeable about their family history, but they also develop a strong feeling of belonging to a group bigger than themselves (aka "intergenerational self")—a group of people who will be there for one another, no matter what, when confronted with life's struggles. The development of the intergenerational self, in turn, leads to greater self-confidence and increased resilience. That's nothing to shake a stick at when you are navigating the tumultuous teen years.

From this research, we know that no matter what you are going through or have been through, if you have the support of a cohesive family unit, you are more likely to have the tools to handle it. The branches of your family tree may not be sheltered from stormy weather, but if you lovingly nourish the roots you came from, the connection and sense of belonging that develop can cause them to flourish even in the most dire conditions.

So carve out time to regularly talk to the members of your extended family about the details of their lives and the positive ways in which they faced hardships. Not only could you pave the way for more personal happiness, but if you pay attention, you might just learn something.

From Disgrace to Delight

As our first teachers, our parents (or other primary caregivers) influence our lives more than anyone else. The loving ones tell us their stories and share their learned wisdom to establish a connection with us and hopefully set us on a path to a future brighter than their own. For my mom, there is one story in particular that she initially told me in my adolescence. A story that came full circle only a few years ago and one that I will always be grateful for.

Born in 1946, my mom was the second oldest of four sisters raised in a very strict Catholic home. They attended mass every day except Saturday. After mass on Sunday, they were quizzed on the gospel to make sure they were all listening. And since it was a sin to eat before receiving Communion, my mom would occasionally pass out at mass.

In this religious context, my mother was taught to be afraid. She grew up with a profound fear of thinking bad thoughts, saying bad words, disagreeing with Catholicism, and having to ultimately pay for her worldly sins in hell. And if one sin was more unforgiveable than the rest for a young Catholic girl during this era, it was premarital sex.

Near the end of my mom's senior year at Purdue University, she found herself happily dating a young man. It was going great until one night when things got out of control. As he held her down, she realized that his desire to have sex was more important to him than her right to say no. She tried to fight him off, but she just didn't have the strength.

In the aftermath of that awful night, my mom was scared. Scared not only of the nightmares that tormented her sleep, but of the hurtful labels, the undeniable disgrace, and the repercussions she feared she would experience if she ended up as a shameful unwed mother, unable to hide what had happened. As she explained to me, in those dark days before women's rights, women who had been sexually abused were anything but victims. The concept of "date rape" had yet to be recognized, so anyone in an established relationship who was having sexual intercourse was considered a willing participant, regardless of how it really happened. Add to the mix a family that kept its issues buried and had difficulties connecting, and it's no surprise that fear was her natural reaction. If her family found out, she knew she would finally be branded the black sheep she had always worried she was— never living up to her older sister's perfection. She didn't feel that she had anyone to go to. She prayed that there would be no ramifications beyond the violation itself, but her fear that God wouldn't answer her prayers was overwhelming. It ended up playing a major role in determining her life path, a path that for decades was for the most part traveled alone.

Approximately four weeks after she was so harshly taken advantage of, my mom went to the student health center and got a blood test. After a very long week waiting for the results, a sympathetic doctor told her she was pregnant—her biggest fear had come true.

Ironically, she remembers walking out of the health center on that beautiful spring day with a smile on her face. No matter the circumstance of the baby's conception, her spirit couldn't contain the inner happiness she felt with the potential for growing a new life inside her. She found the baby's father at work, gave him the news, and not surprisingly, her happiness quickly transformed to sadness. Given how he'd disrespected my mom a month earlier, he predictably didn't pay her any mind. He told her that he didn't believe she was pregnant with his child and went back to his duties at work.

And so her silent journey began.

My mom appreciated the life inside her and knew there were thousands of loving families eager to give a newborn baby a home. Since she couldn't bear the thought of raising a child whose birth would so significantly dishonor herself and her family, and whose conception involved such a painful memory, my mom made plans to give the baby up for adoption. She attended regular appointments at a women's clinic to make sure she and the baby stayed healthy, and she reached out to Catholic Charities. The caring people there not only helped her prepare for the adoption but also found her a job in Chicago and a safe place to live where her condition would remain a secret from the people back home in Indiana.

My mother's family was not unlike many—sharing a space they called home, but keeping the special details of their lives hidden away. If only my mom had been more careful, the details of her pregnancy would've remained hidden as well. Although she usually paid for her visits to the health center with cash, she failed to do so on one occasion. Before my mother left town to start what everyone thought was a new job, her mother beat her to the mailbox on the day that singular bill arrived. After learning the truth, my mom's mother ended up trying to support her daughter through occasional visits to

Illinois and gifts of maternity clothing, but she couldn't offer much more than that—probably due to her own fears.

The day my mother went into labor, she was entirely alone. When she arrived at the hospital, she was wheeled into an area separate from married women also going through labor—so as not to upset *her,* they said.

My mom knew that labor would be difficult, but the hours of physical agony were a cakewalk compared to a heart-wrenching detail she hadn't been warned about—she wouldn't be allowed to hold the baby she had just brought into the world. Her only glimpse of the newborn, whom she named Teresa Marie, was through a glass window to the hospital nursery. Even though she had never questioned her decision to give up the baby, as she truly felt it was the right thing to do, the tears wouldn't stop flowing. She wanted to hold the baby she had carried, even if just for a brief moment, and then hand her over to her future family, who my mother hoped would give her baby a life full of love.

After returning to her family home a few weeks later (after her "job" in Chicago had ended), my mother was faced with something even harder than never holding her newborn child—signing the official paper "irrevocably relinquishing all parental rights to said child." It was a day that started and ended in tears. Lonely tears.

Knowing what my mom went through, alone, breaks my heart. For twenty-five years, she searched for her lost daughter—making phone calls, registering on different adoption sites, filling out multitudes of forms, and updating her contact information anywhere and everywhere she could. In an attempt to help her find solace, I tried on two separate occasions to find my half sister myself. I knew how much my mom yearned to know whether the daughter she had never known was healthy and happy, but neither of us ever heard a peep. No one reached out to us for information. We received no response to our inquiries, and she didn't even have a mother's intuition as to whether her child was still alive.

In December 2008, when "Teresa Marie" was due to celebrate her fortieth birthday, my mother came to the conclusion that she would never know the trajectory her life had taken, and two months later, finally let it go.

A year and a half later, on August 17, 2009, my mom was at work when she picked up a voice-mail message from someone looking to speak with her. Assuming it was job-related, she returned the call.

"This is Roseanne. I believe you were trying to reach me."

She heard: "My name is Kathy. I was born December 30, 1968."

An ordinary call turned into one that couldn't have been more extraordinary.

In shock, my mother sat silently on the phone, wondering if this was the person she had tried to find for more than half of her life or if it was a cruel prank.

"Where were you born?" Mom asked tentatively.

Kathy responded with the correct answer.

That's when the tears started flowing. Once shed from heartbreak, my mother's tears now came from the joy of relief. Over and over again, she said, "Oh my God. Oh my God. Oh my God."

It turns out Kathy had made an inquiry to the Indiana State Department of Health for a medical history. In return, she mistakenly received a letter detailing my mom's full name, address, and phone number. With that information in hand, Kathy did what all amateur sleuths do these days—she turned to Google, a search that overwhelmed her with pages of links referring to the mother of the original Bachelorette. Included in those links were lots of photos, revealing an uncanny resemblance to the woman who was undoubtedly her mother. After discussing it with her boyfriend, Kathy picked up the phone.

Just a couple of days later, my mother and Kathy met face-to-face for the first time, realizing that they lived only a few hours apart. I wasn't able to be there, but as the girl whose name had been changed from Teresa Marie to Kathy described to me, "It was open arms, *everywhere!*" My family embraced Kathy as one of their own, because that's what she is.

Once in turmoil over the cards she had been dealt and her decision about how to play them, my mom was now content with her unanswered prayers. As Helen Keller once said, "The struggle of life is one of our greatest blessings. It makes us patient, sensitive, and Godlike. It teaches us that although the world is full of suffering, it is also full of the overcoming of it." It took forty years, but the relief was well worth the wait. My mom is now bonded to a daughter she thought she would never meet and in the process has taught so much to all of us who know her story (myself included). With her help, I learned to keep moving forward in the face of life's hardships, to know that things happen as they are supposed to, and to be grateful for the bumpy road that leads to happy hearts.

TAKEN TOO SOON

Even as a hopeful optimist who attempts to live with a heart full of gratitude, I am also a realist who recognizes the difference between bumpy roads and roads with bumps so abrupt and massive that finding a way over them can seem impossible. Losing a loved one definitely fits into the latter category and is something I experienced firsthand as a teenager when I unexpectedly lost my cousin Chip.

Chip had a smile that could light up the night and a heart that was even brighter. He was a playful and mischievous soul who could get away with just about anything by batting the enviable eyelashes that framed his beautiful blue eyes. Full of energy and laughter, he was a lover of life—right up until his life came to a sudden end.

I'll never forget that day. It was the weekend and I had one goal—to sleep as late as possible. Awaiting the start of my sophomore year of college, I was wasting away as much of the summer as I could before I had to hunker down and figure out what I wanted to be when I grew up. I remember the sun blazing through my windows, but I had no intention of coming out from under my warm and cozy covers. That changed in an instant when I heard my mom's frenzied voice on the phone.

My grandfather had called to say that my twenty-one-year-young cousin Chip had been involved in an accident during a go-kart race and taken to the nearest hospital. After nearly a day of agonizing waiting, we found out that it was just a matter of time before Chip's body succumbed to his injuries. So, as soon as we could, we made our way to Indiana.

I remember cautiously approaching Chip's room in the ICU. I had been warned about his appearance, but nothing could prepare me for what I saw. The swelling of his head was so severe that the man I knew and the cousin I loved was completely unrecognizable. Even though he had had safety on his side with a fire suit and helmet, it just hadn't been enough to protect his brain against the irreversible damage that occurred during the collision on the Crawfordsville race-track. Two days later, on June 29, 1992, the machines keeping Chip alive were turned off, and his physical presence in our lives came to an almost unbearable end.

The final image of him is something my mind will never be able to erase, but the disturbing visual of his frail and un-recognizable body was only a fraction of the reason I was so deeply affected.

Until that summer, I thought accidents happened to other people. My cousin was in the prime of his life. He was a good person with a good heart, and he had taken every precau-tion he could to stay safe while following his passion. He was happy. He was alive. He was preparing to propose to his long-time girlfriend and start a family of his own. Then, in what felt like the blink of an eye, his life on earth was over, just as mine could be the next day or the day after that.

With Chip's death, I was closer to mortality than ever before—it was frightening. As a young adult, I could com-prehend what it meant to die, but I had a profoundly dif-ficult time dealing with the death of a close relative who should've been decades away from it. I tried to stay strong for the ones who had known him best and loved him most, but couldn't always deny the pain and would literally end up in the fetal position. I cried for my loss, but even more than that, I cried for my grandparents, who thought they would pass on before their grandchildren; my cousin, who didn't get the chance to say good-bye to her only sibling; and my aunt and uncle, who would never again hug the son they had given life to.

That summer I became even more stifled by caution and fear than I had been for most of my life. I realized more than ever before that, even in moments of assumed safety, the surrounding world was far beyond my control. To this day, it affects my actions as well as my parenting. Even though I try to put the brakes on my fears, they are difficult to overcome when they are buried so deeply into my soul.

Thankfully, though, that devastating summer also taught me a lot.

For one, I realized that no matter how fervently you believe in heaven above, or how strong you appear to those around you, nothing can or should prevent you from expressing your anguish when faced with the end of a beautiful life. It isn't weakness that shows through during emotional expression, but the raw beauty of humanity.

Another positive effect was the undeniable transformation that took place within our family. Previously disconnected, my mother, her three sisters, and their parents accepted that their vulnerability wasn't a sign of weakness and opened their hearts in shared grief. Through their struggle, they developed a true bond offering one another a level of unconditional support that they still maintain to this day. Their example showed me that sometimes nature has to rattle your core to help you find your own strength as well as the strength of those who will hold you high above your hurdles.

Lastly, experiencing death made me understand the treasure of life at a very young age. When I was nineteen, my thoughts revolved around college courses and rushing the best sorority, but after losing Chip, I gained the gift of awareness. Today was a gift. My health was a gift. Every breath I took was a gift. I am the first to admit that I still need constant reminders to slow down and embrace my blessings, often literally, but after losing an angel to heaven too soon, I knew the importance of focusing on the precious gift of the here and now.

Since that devastating day in 1992, there have been many times I've randomly felt my cousin's presence in a room. I know I won't have a chance to see him in the flesh again, but in those unexplained moments I am overcome with gratitude for just having known him. In the words of Dr. Seuss: "Don't cry because it's over. Smile because it happened"—and, in remembering the blessing of my cousin, that's exactly what I do.

THE BIG PICTURE

On the heels of the heartbreaking ordeals above, I hesitate to share a story that, looking back, seems so incredibly silly. But just as important as life-altering events are to the way we choose to live, so are the trivial stressors we face on a daily basis. Both influence our choices, attitudes, actions, and levels of happiness, even if they seem completely incomparable in terms of significance.

January 24, 2013, was one of those seemingly insignificant days. With a looming deadline, I realized that I needed help with my mommy duties and practically begged my mother-in-law to stay with us for a bit. As the quintessential doting grandparent, she happily agreed and headed to our nest in the mountains for what ended up being twelve days. I know many of you may cringe at the thought of your mother-in-law in your home for almost two weeks, but around here her visits are highly anticipated, for multiple reasons.

First and foremost, Barb is a model mother—very patient, always nurturing, and unconditionally supportive.

Second, she is an exceptional grandmother. Our children absolutely adore her, so much so that I often hear "No, Mommy, I want Grandma to . . . "

Third, she is pretty much the perfect homemaker, and she loves it. I don't think I've ever seen a speck of dust in her always white-glove-ready home, a hamper overflowing with dirty clothing, a bed not made, a guest towel out of place, or a full and delicious meal not ready to be devoured when the clock strikes 5:30 p.m. And she treats our home as she does her own, with lots of love and attention.

We feel truly blessed that Ryan's parents live only a couple hours away, and we reach out for their help when the need arises, which ends up being at least once a month. We love their company, feel thankful that they can usually get away on a moment's notice, value the bond they are able to consistently create with their first grandbabies, and know our kids are in some of the most dependable and loving hands possible. For the most part, our visits go smoothly, and this one wasn't any different—that is, until two days before she was due to head home.

That morning, I was awakened in the middle of a dream (or, should I say, nightmare) by my sweet baby girl softly saying, "Mommy," in my ear. I couldn't get rid of the horrible image my mind had conjured up of Ryan saying a particularly romantic good-bye to a very tall and very pretty girl. The worst part: he looked right at me and did nothing. No remorse.

I knew it wasn't real, and Blakesley couldn't have been sweeter or calmer, but it started my day off on the completely wrong foot.

In an attempt to shift my dark mood, I held my daughter's tiny hand as we walked downstairs, in hopes that her grasp would be a conduit for positive energy. Then we headed to the kitchen to get the day started with breakfast and making school lunches.

As I walked down the stairs, I noticed my mother-in-law struggling with something in the sink. I asked what was wrong. She explained that she was trying to get one of the kids' cups unstuck from under the little black skirt of the disposal.

Still foggy from my face-to-face with Ryan and his new friend back in dreamland, I said something to the effect of, "Huh? How'd that happen?"

I knew it wasn't something she did on purpose, but after starting off the morning on a bad note, I was frustrated, and the tone of my voice probably conveyed that.

Even more frustrated than me (considering she had been dealing with the annoyance of this stuck cup), she answered, "Well, I don't know, Trista."

My frustration immediately started to snowball.

I tried anything and everything I could—including a knife, a saw, a Shop-Vac, and even a Super Glued stick—to get the wedged cup from blocking the sink.

Nothing worked.

With Ryan not returning from an ice-climbing rescue class until the next day, I called some friends to ask for the name of a fair-priced local plumber. I knew my father-in-law would be there later that day, but feeling impatient, I wanted a professional to come in and pull the cup out from under the sink as soon as possible. Having required the help of the pros years ago, I knew it wouldn't be a cheap visit, which made me even more frustrated. Worse, I felt disrespected—and it killed me.

It wasn't the feelings I was having that were beating me down. It was the fact that the feelings were directed at a woman who had such love for our family, and for me, that she had agreed to come to the chaos of my house and offer a kind of support that I couldn't ask of anyone else.

A woman I consistently feel I don't measure up to.

A woman so kind and thoughtful that I can't imagine anyone associating her with anything bad. She was an angel, so by the power of my mind's deduction, I was the devil, and the day just spiraled from there.

With the kids at school and my mother-in-law visiting with the friends she had made here, I wasted the day crying and thinking about what a sucky human I was.

My father-in-law eventually arrived and expertly freed the cup from the sink. In the end, there was no need for a plumber, or a wasted day, for that matter. A cup had gotten stuck.

Big. Freaking. Deal.

When Ryan got home the next day, he reminded me of the big picture. In a twelve-day period with a three- and five-year-old and a stressed-out writer under deadline, a sink accident was a small price to pay for all the immense help and productivity his mother had allowed. She had dropped everything in her life to offer a generous helping hand, and what was important was that I had a peaceful avenue to attempt to catch up on work without neglecting my kids.

At the end of a day that started so horribly, I learned three great lessons:

1. If a sink breaks, you have a broken sink. So what. It's just a sink.
2. Appliances are easily repaired or replaced. Relationships are not, especially those that come from pure love and consistently fill our bank of blessings.

3. I need to take a page out of my own book and remember to focus on gratitude, especially in stressful times.

Happily Ever Actions

≈ To stay connected to our family living thousands of miles from each other, my mom set up a Facebook group just for us. It includes my half sister, my aunts, and my cousins and is a way for all of us to tune in to some of the most important people of our lives. If you're feeling particularly detached from your loved ones, try doing the same and start the ball of reconnection rolling.

≈ It can be immensely difficult to share your true emotions with the people you love, but after being faced with the fact that life is fleeting, I can say that it's worth every uncomfortable moment. Start with the people you struggle with the most. Maybe it's a parent, grandparent, or sibling. Before you finish your next conversation with that person, try out these three simple words: "I love you." If that seems like too much to take on, maybe start signing your e-mails "Love," and then gradually work into "love ya" then "I love you." If you are worried about rejection or nonreciprocation, just think about the fact that you may not have the same chance tomorrow, and go for it. Nothing is stronger or more powerfully binding than a pure statement of love.

All in the Extended Family

☞ Unless you're really lucky, your extended family is scattered across the country, or even the globe. The beauty of the twenty-first century, though, is that technology is ready and waiting for you to use it to your advantage to reach out and connect with someone. A call via Skype or Facetime or even the old-fashioned telephone doesn't really compare to a kiss or a hug, but it's better than nothing, and letting them know how much you care can put smiles on the faces of those you love.

☞ To develop a family full of members with a strong sense of intergenerational self, sit down without distraction and talk. It's as simple as that and can happen whenever and wherever focused attention is possible. Maybe it's during mealtime or snack time, while at celebrations or on vacations. Regardless of the where, make time for the what. You'll not only be spending quality time making memories, but you'll be setting the stage for a strong family unit that communicates effectively and lives happily.

Thank You for Being a Friend

True friendship multiplies the good in life and divides its evils. Strive to have friends, for life without friends is like life on a desert island . . . to find one real friend in a lifetime is good fortune; to keep him is a blessing.

—BALTASAR GRACIAN

CHAPTER SIX

I GREW UP IN SUBURBAN CHESTERFIELD, MISSOURI, WHERE my mom, my dad, our black Lab, Abbey, and I lived a relatively happy life—that is, until my parents sat me down one surprising evening when I was in fifth grade and asked if I knew what "divorce" meant. Of course I had heard of it, but even after witnessing them argue for years, I never thought I would experience this devastating family upheaval firsthand. All these years later, I understand that they made the best decision for themselves and for our family, and our lives are better for it. I will admit, though, that when their marriage officially ended, I was incredibly sad.

As a little girl, it was one of the hardest things I had to deal with, both emotionally and logistically. After a judge weighed in, I was required to pack a bag every other weekend and travel thirty minutes to my dad's house. That half hour felt like forever to me. As a mother who wants nothing more than to spend time with her kids, I understand why it was important for me to go, but back then it was the last thing I wanted to spend my Saturdays and Sundays doing. Instead of seeing those weekends as an opportunity to bond with my dad—whom I would now be ecstatic to see more often—I was solely focused on the fact that I was missing out on time with my friends. Big slumber party? I would miss it. Lounging by my BFF's pool? Nope. Sunday at the movies? With my dad, maybe, but not with the girls, who I knew were clustered together over a barrel of popcorn, laughing their heads off and creating memories that I wouldn't be a part of. Since I was an only child, my friends were the sisters I didn't have (at least until later in life when I was blessed with both a stepsister and a half sister). And especially for a teenager, nothing quite compares to time with your friends. So even though I've always loved my dad, those weekends just about broke my heart.

When I think back on my childhood, those feelings of closeness, of belonging, of a connection with friends spring to mind. I remember the afternoons we spent giggling at the mall. Late-night phone calls sobbing about the boys who had broken our hearts. Lunchtime in the cafeteria at school, laughing about everything and absolutely nothing. I've always had such a deep appreciation for my friends, and that will never change. I love Ryan, my children, and my entire extended family, but my friends give me something my family can't. They are my trusted therapists, pick-me-ups, and sounding boards who have usually been able to empathize with my struggles and successes best because most of them are at the same point in life that I am. They keep me company on the phone when my house is empty, share wise counsel about birthday-party and outfit planning, offer to pick up the kids from school if I have the flu, and remind me of what really matters when life hits a rough patch.

If you're anything like me, you strive to be nurturing, considerate, and loyal, but sometimes it's easy to take friends for granted. Take, for example, this story of Michelle (or, as I call her, Miss), my best friend from graduate school. She had just given birth to her first- *and* secondborn—twin baby girls named Carolina and Daniella. Born prematurely at twenty-seven weeks and at a little over a pound each, they were fighting for their lives in the neonatal intensive care unit of Joe DiMaggio Children's Hospital. Her friends and family offered immeasurable support during that extremely difficult time, but what struck her the most was the thoughtfulness and unconditional devotion of three women: Beth, Penny, and Elizabeth.

Miss had been friendly with these women through her job as a physical therapist in the rehabilitation department at Memorial Regional, the sister hospital to Joe DiMaggio Children's, prior to her admission on the labor and delivery floor there. However, their interactions had always been limited to the workplace.

Until now.

These three were the first visitors Michelle had in the recovery room after her traumatic C-section, and they stuck around for every step of her family's two-and-a-half-month journey, always stopping by to check on them before, during, and after breaks on their shifts on the rehab floor. They offered listening ears as well as comforting shoulders to cry on when Miss needed them most. On one noteworthy occasion, Elizabeth showed up at the hospital at 1:00 a.m. after one of Michelle's baby girls had undergone an especially difficult surgery. Michelle had called to vent and Elizabeth came to sit and just be her friend. She didn't have to say anything. Just showing up and being emotionally present was enough.

Throughout the experience, Michelle thanked her lucky stars that those ladies stepped up when it really counted. I counted mine too. Living more than 2,000 miles away, I flew in to be by Miss's side for what seemed like a blip of a visit, but at least when I left I knew she was in capable, caring hands, and my guilt dissipated (slightly).

The four women no longer work together, but Michelle has remained friends with them all. She knows that Elizabeth, Penny, and Beth all would drop everything again to be there for her, come what may, as she would be for each of them. She learned that even though she expected her family and closest friends to show their unadulterated support, she should never overlook those in her life with whom she may not have a long history, but who nonetheless want to be a dedicated part of her life. Taking her friends for granted isn't an option. It shouldn't be for any of us either.

MAKE NEW FRIENDS BUT KEEP THE OLD

Francesco Guicciardini, an Italian historian, said, "Since there is nothing so well worth having as friends, never lose a chance to make them." It is a lesson even my young son, Max, could take to heart.

Max has always been sweetly shy, even when he was a baby. He lights up around his buddies and people he has a history with, but in new situations with unfamiliar faces, he has a difficult time sticking his neck out. June 18, 2012, was one of those days.

We had enrolled four-year-old Max in a weeklong sports camp called "Mini Hawks," which they do in our area every summer. On opening day, we dropped him off for what we thought we would be three hours of fun-filled playtime. He would learn about basketball, baseball, and soccer, happily put more miles on his size-ten sneakers, and maybe even make some friends. That's what we hoped, at least.

From the time I picked him up at the end of the day, and throughout the evening, I noticed that he was "off." I couldn't put my finger on it, but I suspected that he was either exhausted from running around all day, starting to come down with a nasty bug, or something was making him sad.

At bedtime, Ryan and I said goodnight to Blakesley first, and then it was Max's turn to be tucked in. After he crawled under his covers, I said, "As your mommy, I will always be here to listen. Can you tell me why you are sad?"

He looked at me with his big, beautiful hazel eyes and quietly said, "No one would play with me today."

My. Heart. Broke.

For a parent, hearing that your child is hurting is one of the most emotionally painful experiences you can experience. I felt my heart tearing into pieces for him. He hadn't been bullied or beaten or physically hurt, but of all the experiences he'd had in his four years of life, this one made him feel miserable. Normally partnered up with his lively little sister or his best friend, Knox, whom he met when he was five days old in the neonatal intensive care unit, he had never felt the crushing sensation of feeling alone on a field full of his peers.

I immediately went into glass-half-full mode and suggested that maybe since Knox hadn't signed up for the camp, Max could try to make a special new friend the next day. Maybe even one he could introduce Knox to and they could all play together.

His face lit up as he said, "Yeah!"

I explained that I knew it was hard for him to talk to boys and girls he didn't know, but if he tried, he might meet someone he could have a super-fun day with. Besides, his daddy and I were partially to blame because we had arrived a few minutes late that morning, and the campers had already gone through the round of introductions.

Determined to make tomorrow a better day, Max went to sleep that night with a smile on his face and hope in his heart for a new friend. I could only pray that it would come to fruition.

Driving to Donovan Park to pick him up after camp the next day, I could feel my heart pounding in my chest. I searched the basketball court where they had the kids line up to wait for their parents to take them home and spotted Max—laughing. An instantaneous smile shot across my face.

When the counselors called Max's name, he grabbed the backpack filled with extra clothes that was nearly half his size and came running toward Blakesley and me.

"Mommy, I made a new friend!"

I will never forget those joyful words or the abundance of pride I saw in my son's expression.

After a day of heartache, he had soared above his expectations and met a boy he to this day calls his friend. With their ability to make each other laugh and a shared interest in swimming, ice-skating, T-ball, and being all-around silly, these two little boys had begun what hopefully will be a friendship that will continue for years and years to come.

To Be(friend) or Not to Be(friend)

"I didn't come here to make friends."

If you have ever watched *The Bachelor* or *The Bachelorette,* you've heard that phrase at least once every season. Some resolute contestants start down the fantasy date-filled path focusing all their energy on the road to a spouse, rather than the road to new friends. As someone who turned thirty during her televised quest for Prince Charming, I get that mind-set—I wanted a husband! The contestants think that if they actively ignore the other participants and focus solely on the man (or woman) of the hour, it will give them a leg up on the competition and they'll be that much closer to the end of the fairy-tale rainbow.

Maybe. But I say, as with any other life experience, what would it hurt to turn strangers into friends? As Rod McKuen, an American singer-songwriter and poet, has said, "Strangers are just friends waiting to happen."

Granted, when I first applied for *The Bachelor,* I wanted some excitement, to escape the rut I was feeling bogged down in, to travel, and perhaps most important, to meet some new friends. I've never understood the whole "I didn't come here to make friends" strategy. Yes, everyone is vying for the same person, but by isolating yourself and being unfriendly, you aren't showing your love interest that you are more dedicated to finding a partner—you are just showing him or her you are unfriendly and like to be socially isolated. To me, finding love in this (yes, unconventional) way has always been about showing your true colors and hoping that the compatibility pieces fall into place.

Granted, in ancient times, when I appeared on the first season of *The Bachelor,* all of the contestants, including myself, were naive. Even though we were explicitly told by the producers that we were in competition with one another, we were still just trying to find our footing in an unusual (albeit luxurious) environment. So we made it simple: when we weren't out with our bachelor, we enjoyed our temporary lavish digs in paradise, had all-hours gab sessions, and whiled away our days by the pool with our fourteen new friends (on the first season, fifteen of us moved into the mansion after the first rose ceremony).

In the most recent seasons, I get that it's not that simple. Many of the participants come into the process with a one-track mind—they want to stroll off into the sunset with a Neil Lane diamond on their ring finger. They want to be the next Ashley and J.P. or even Ryan and Trista. Since it's not just them and their potential soul mate going through the courtship process as they would in the real world, this naturally causes a bit of drama. And I've never seen a producer fail to give existent drama a little nudge in the even-more-drama direction. After all, it's the producers' job to create attention-grabbing television and use anything they can to get America and the world to watch, even if that means encouraging rivalries, as opposed to allegiances, among the competitors.

The contestants think: Why make a friend with someone who is supposedly my enemy?

My response: Why not?

Even if you go on the show looking to fall in love, falling into like with some new friends isn't such a bad thing.

I can attest to that.

More than eleven years after we said our televised good-byes, there are four girls out of those fourteen original roommates I still call my friends: Shannon, Amy, Angelique, and Christina. That's pretty good odds. Each of them has gone on to find her own happily ever after in Texas, England, and California, but I will always look back at the laughter we shared in that big ol' beautiful house on Zuma Beach and be thankful that those women were with me. None of us won the heart of the man we all were vying for, but I'd say we all came out winners.

THE POWER OF HOPE

When I announced to my friends, family, and fans that I would be writing this book, the congratulatory messages I received were a very sweet, and welcome, surprise. Some of the most cherished notes came from loving friends who reached out with personal words of thanks. One of those friends was Amy Madden Copp.

Amy is a longtime friend of the Sutters, and when I became a Sutter myself, we hit it off and I felt lucky to then call her a friend, as well. Amy is a fun-loving and kind social butterfly with a happy soul. That happiness was temporarily threatened, however, when her attempts at becoming a mother proved to be more difficult than she had expected.

Her spirit seemed indestructible, but early in 2009 she shared with me her struggles, which created an immediate bond of commonality between us. I told her the story of my own disappointments in trying to conceive and that, just like me and millions of others, she should never give up hope.

She never did.

On August 25, 2009, she gave birth to a beauty named Maddy Noel.

Three years later, when I announced that I would be writing a book about having a grateful heart, Amy wrote me this message on Facebook: "Congrats, Trista! This is exciting. I think of you often when you encouraged me to keep trying for a baby. The miracle that is Maddy is a result of encouragement from my friends and your positive attitude that day! Gratitude all the way around!"

Although I humbly accept that I played a teeny-tiny part in her unrelenting resolve to continue moving forward toward achieving her personal dreams, I have it on good authority that the birds and the bees and a higher power played the predominant role in her pregnancy. I think it's also fair to say that, without an already mostly positive attitude toward life and the support of her wonderful family and friends, my conversation with her that night would've had a good chance of falling to the wayside.

Many who endure the pain of unanswered prayers aren't as lucky as Amy. They feel alone and ignored. They don't have the self-confidence to believe in the realization of their life's goals. They have no hope.

Some may say and have said that that's a good thing. Take Sophocles, a Greek playwright, for example. He believed that human suffering was prolonged by hope. And the philosopher Plato thought that hope was a "foolish counselor." Well, I'm not an ancient Grecian, a legendary playwright, or a brilliant philosopher, but my simple thought is that without hope, we are hopeless. I'm happy to be the kind of person to encourage hope in my friends and vice versa. With the help of that encouragement, I'm able to live a life of optimistic possibility, rather than bleak impossibility. I'd say that's a much better scenario, wouldn't you?

Science thinks so. In studies conducted by the late C. R. Snyder, an author and professor of clinical psychology, it was found that hope is directly associated with increased coping skills, improved performance in academics and sports, and higher levels of self-esteem, satisfaction, optimism, meaning in life, and happiness (even taking into account genetic predispositions for success in these areas).

So, in my logical mind, friends encourage hope, hope fosters happiness, and happiness inspires gratitude (at least it did with my friend Amy). Just one more reason to never give up hope and to always cherish your friends.

LOST . . . AND FOUND

On December 24, 2012, I sat in the huge new barn at 4 Eagle Ranch in Wolcott, Colorado, intently listening to the Cowboy Christmas sermon by our friend Pastor Tommy Schneider. Pastor Tommy has such a way with words that he could probably tell me about how paint dries and I would be fascinated, but I think most of the hundreds who joined me that day will agree that the story of Reject, the buffalo, stood out as particularly captivating.

I hope you like it too. . . .

On an especially stormy, lightning-filled night on a private Colorado ranch back in 1991, a baby buffalo was born. Whether it was the traumatic weather or the mother passed out and woke up to an unrecognizable calf, we'll never know. For whatever reason, he was abandoned—first by his own mother, and second by her herd, which followed her lead. Had it not been for the knowledgeable ranch hands who expertly intervened that night, the young buffalo wouldn't have needed a name, as he very easily could've died that day . . . either due to the lack of maternal protection from outside predators, or the natural tendency of a herd to kill an animal they think of as an outsider. Instead, the people at the ranch kept him safe from harm and from that day forward, he was known as Reject.

Until he was about six months old, they bottle-fed him, but then he simply became too large for them to handle, so the nearby 4 Eagle Ranch accepted him as part of their clan.

Right around the time Reject turned a year old, he was put in the same pen as another animal his age—Snowflake, the horse. With an injured leg, Snowflake could never be the trail horse they had planned for her to be. Instead of selling her, though, they decided to test the waters by putting the two lonesome animals together, and it was magic. As DeWayne Davis, the ranch's general manager, explained to me, it is *really* unusual for a buffalo and a horse to bond, but that's exactly what happened. "They are pretty much inseparable."

And that's the case with just about any animal that happens to be sharing space with Reject, be it a goat, a burro, or an alpaca. He has found friends at 4 Eagle Ranch, and in return they have found a protector. As is usually the case in that neck of the woods, coyotes are a big problem, preying on most of the animals that call the ranch their home, but with Reject keeping watch over his friends, the coyotes don't show their furry faces.

As Pastor Tommy said at Cowboy Christmas, Reject had a purpose and a reason for suffering. He found his way to 4 Eagle and Snowflake and a happy life playing guardian to his diverse group of buddies. As Anaïs Nin, an American author, said, "Each friend represents a world in us, a world possibly not born until they arrive, and it is only by this meeting that a new world is born."

Yes, Reject is a buffalo, but we can all learn from his path to unlikely friendships.

FURRY FRIENDS

What is the definition of "friend"? The Merriam-Webster online dictionary says: "one attached to another by affection or esteem." In our household, we would expand it to say: one attached to another by affection or esteem *regardless of species.* If they walk on all fours, like to play fetch, have a tail, or are covered with fur, our pets earn the title of friend quite easily.

Since I've been with Ryan, we've always had a fur baby in our home. Whether cozied up for a nighttime snuggle, greeting you at the door with a wagging tail, or playfully nudging a chew toy your way so you will start a game of tug-of-war, our dogs are always there for us. That is, until they aren't.

The blogs below were written for Buzz.Snow.com in November 2011—the month our thirteen-year-old Siberian husky, Natasha (aka Tosh), took her last breath. The first is by the talented writer I call my husband, and the second was written by me. Different in content, they both depict the genuine appreciation we felt for the time Tosh gave us here on earth and how she will always be with us, as a true friend should.

Lessons from a Snow Dog

by Ryan Sutter

Thirteen years ago, I met my dog, Natasha. Thirteen days ago, I said goodbye to her for the last time.

I had no intention of getting a dog when I first met her. I simply saw her for sale on the side of the road and, without thought or hesitation, added her to my life. In turn, what she added to my life would prove to be the guiding principles from which my current philosophies and attitude were crafted.

Dogs are special creatures. Their presence in life is the root of both profound happiness and sadness. Living almost exclusively for the moment, a dog's love is undiluted by the past or future. Natasha saw me through the most turbulent and tumultuous times of my life. Never has there been a period of more profound change than the time we shared together. Yet through it all, she remained loyal with a patience and calm that would seem condescending were they not rooted entirely in love. Her adventurous spirit fostered my relationship with the mountains and secured them as the place I now and forever will call home.

Natasha was a source of security and comfort. When we hiked, she would look back to make sure I was still coming and OK. Her ability to ensure safety without an overbearing concern for the possibility of danger has been incorporated into my parenting techniques. Her ability to summon energy and enthusiasm despite her age and pain is the source of inspiration that solicits my many varied escapades. The comfort and solace I seek and feel in nature echoes her wild spirit and channels the love of the outdoor lifestyle we both shared. Natasha's simple notions reflected her pure understanding of life and provided a constant source of stability to my often wobbly existence. Her obvious love of the Vail Valley cemented my residential fate. I am here because of her.

Dogs speak in a language of action not words. They cannot lie. Their eyes are truly the windows to their soul. I will never forget the life reflected in Natasha's eyes. Nor will I ever forget the day that life left. A dog comes into your life, makes it better and then leaves. Though I miss her profoundly, I am forever grateful for the happiness she brought. My life is better for her having been in it.

Trista Sutter Says Good-bye to
Her Best Friend's Best Friend

by Trista Sutter

As a gift for my husband, I once had our Siberian husky, Natasha's, image put into a photo frame inscribed "The Love of My Life." After all, Natasha had been there for Ryan during his most tumultuous times. She had an unbreakable and beautiful bond with him that I could only hope to share, but when I first met her, I didn't know if she would ever let me. Granted, their four-year love affair with the Vail Valley had been rudely interrupted when Ryan suddenly (at least in Natasha's mind) disappeared for a few weeks, and then again when he showed up with a strange, allergy-ridden girl who couldn't touch her without getting instantaneous hives. Add to that the bright lights and a treat-less camera crew.

As someone who considers herself loyal and protective of the people I love, I could understand the reluctance and warnings I saw in her piercing blue eyes. She happily welcomed any love I gave her, but I knew there was a line she was wary of any woman crossing . . . any woman who could potentially break her best friend's heart again.

Nine years to the day later, we found out that our "pretty girl" would be given her angel wings. Trying to make her final hours on Earth as happy as possible, Ryan took her for one last hike in the gorgeous mountains that she had called home—her favorite thing to do with her favorite person. Upon their return, I headed outside to welcome them home.

I wrapped my arms around Ryan, then kneeled down to Tosh's level to pet the especially soft spot between her eyes, just as I had done thousands of times before. As I looked into those crystal-blue soul windows, I assumed I would see the same confusion and fear we had so abruptly started to notice in that last week, but instead she gazed back at me and licked my nose—twice. She had kissed me many times before, but this was different. For that brief moment, she wasn't frightened or in pain. She knew exactly where she was, whom she was with, and what she needed to do to help her adopted mommy through one of the hardest days of her life. In that wet kiss (which oddly enough never gave me hives), I felt her unconditional love and acceptance—the acceptance I had worried I would never earn. It was a surprise gift I will cherish forever. She was telling me that it was okay. She knew that her best friend was in loving and protective hands and she was ready to go. She had had a wonderful life and she was thankful I had been part of it. I just hope she knew that the feeling was mutual.

HERE'S TO YOUR HEALTH

I don't know about you, but my friends (including those of the furry variety) fulfill more than just the role of sidekick in my life. Recently I learned that friends actually fulfill another very important role: they make us healthier. The Mayo Clinic says that having friends can increase our sense of belonging and purpose, which in turn makes us happier and decreases our stress levels. Friends help us through difficult life changes, and encourage us to drop unhealthy habits like skipping the gym and wallowing in a bottle of wine. Sure, most of us know this instinctively, but now the research proves it: friends are the stuff of a long and happy life. And it's not only the Mayo Clinic offering official medical support for keeping buddies around. Check out these findings and then go call a friend (or give him or her a pet on the belly)!

- In 2006, the American Society of Clinical Oncology published research from a study of nearly 3,000 nurses who had breast cancer. What they learned was that those without close friends were four times more likely to die of the disease than those with close friends, no matter how near or far their friends lived. And maybe even more interesting to note, compared to friends, having a spouse wasn't connected to survival rates of those studied. Puts a little more meaning into "girl power," right?
- In 1997, Sheldon Cohen, a professor at Carnegie Mellon University, did a study that ended up in the *Journal of the American Medical Association*. They reported that the incidence of colds in 276 people between the ages of eighteen and fifty-five was significantly reduced by the number and diversity of their social relationships. More friends in greater categories = fewer colds. I'm ready to make some new friends. Are you?
- In 2001, Dr. Redford B. Williams and other researchers at Duke University Medical Center reported that people with heart disease were six times more likely to die within six months if their social ties were in short supply. I hope to never suffer from heart disease, but I'm thinking a little proactive dedication to my friends can't hurt.
- There are many reasons pet owners (including myself) embrace the chance to give a dog or cat or lizard or bird—or whatever may suit their style—a home, and if health benefits aren't on their list, they should

be, according to the multitude of studies that have recently flooded the scientific community. WebMD. com reviewed a gaggle of them, including some from the American Cancer Society, CDC, American Diabetes Association, and *Psychology Today,* reporting that animal companionship can increase serotonin production, thereby lessening stress, lower blood pressure, improve cardiac function, strengthen children's immune systems, and improve the owner's overall quality of life. I've always loved my furry friends, but now with this research, I love them even more!

HAPPILY EVER ACTIONS

A few years after we graduated college, five of my sorority sisters and I decided that because we were scattering around the country and didn't want to miss out on one another's daily lives, we would circulate a journal between us. We filled it with photos as well as our latest personal successes and challenges, and waited eagerly until it was our turn to get the scoop in the mail. "The Journal" (as we called it) ceased after we all started having babies, but I've made an executive decision to reinstate it. I miss my girls and want to keep our friendship chain going for a long time to come. If you feel the same about your long-lost besties, join us in revving up the postal system again. Find a light journal that's easy to mail, figure out the chain of delivery, get to writing, and wait. The smiles and the revived connection will come, I promise.

≈ Life is busy. We all get wrapped up in the daily grind, which makes it hard to maintain stable relationships with our friends, but it doesn't have to be so difficult. Sometimes short and sweet and present is better than fabulous yet forced. From a kindhearted comment posted to one of their pictures on Facebook to a brief phone call while you're making dinner or a short trip to the nail salon for side-by-side polish changes, even the smallest gestures will let you both reap the friendship benefits.

≈ When I first moved to Vail, I had a hard time meeting girlfriends. It took me a good five years, birthing my first child, and attending "Mommy and Me" classes with ladies who were as tired, inexperienced, in love, and ecstatic as I was. We bonded over the commonality of being freshly labeled a proud parent, and I realized I should've put more thought into introducing myself to like-minded people when I first became a resident of the Vail Valley. When I made the move, I took a dance class here and there, and hit the gym every so often, but I was in and out in a flash and usually wearing headphones while working out. In hindsight, I know I should've branched out and tried to make new friends, just as I asked my son to do years later. I should've joined organizations or taken part in hobbies that would introduce me to people I shared common interests and life paths with, more so than I actually did. If you find yourself in the same boat, don't do as I did. Put yourself out there. Get involved in your community—in the things that bring a smile to your face. Give yourself the chance to meet a new pal, and when a friendship sticks, tell that person how grateful you are to have him or her in your life. If commonality is the attraction, gratitude is the glue.

Every year at Christmas, I send out about three hundred Christmas cards, and we get about that many in return. Wanting to showcase the happy faces of our friends and family every winter in our home, I decided about seven years back to start taping them to our pantry doorway. They now take up not only that, but the side of a cabinet as you come up our entry stairs. Around April or May, I start feeling like holiday cards may not be appropriate decor, but I usually push it back because I love seeing the smiles of the growing families of my very missed friends. Whether it's a week or a month or half of the year, find a place to display those cherished faces and don't apologize for wanting to have a visual reminder of your blessed friendships to anyone. I don't.

Never enter a new experience thinking, "I didn't come here to make friends." Open your mind and your heart, and think about the true friendships of your life. Had you closed off your mind and isolated yourself from getting to know anyone new, would you still be able to call them your pals? As the actress Shirley MacLaine once said, "Fear makes strangers of people who would be friends." Don't let fear or stubbornness or a bad attitude keep possible friendships at bay. You deserve friendship. You deserve one of the greatest joys of life.

The Business
of Being Happy

Do not be fooled.

Success is not the key to happiness.

Happiness is the key to success.

—ANONYMOUS

CHAPTER SEVEN

HAVE YOU EVER BEEN AT WORK AND FELT SO ANGRY that you could swear your head grew horns, your eyes grew daggers, and your ears puffed out smoke? Maybe you felt so blindsided by a superior's criticism that you felt like a smashed bug on the bottom of their shoe?

My husband certainly has—on the day he was hired by the Vail Fire Department. After working as a resident there for ten months, Ryan finally got the offer for a full-time position. He was thrilled, at least until the fire chief he would be working under decided to share his blatant honesty. "Just so you know," Ryan remembers him saying, "you weren't my choice. I don't believe that guys with college degrees will last very long. I don't think you'll be successful here." Talk about laying out the unwelcome mat.

Undeterred, Ryan stuck to his guns, and now, after ten years and a steady climb up the ladder, he eventually achieved his current rank of lieutenant. He sure proved his old boss wrong! But I know for a fact that Ryan didn't work as hard as he did because of that negative incentive. It's in his bones and his blood and his upbringing to be the best he can be. I can only imagine, though, how much more fulfilled he would've felt all these years if he'd had the chief's support . . . or had at least been spared the knowledge of his utter disappointment.

At work, just as much as at home, everyone needs and wants to feel valued. Whether it's taking out the trash, asking a client to hold while his or her call is connected, or ringing up a customer's purchases, all jobs are important, and every employee should be recognized for his or her hard work and dedication. Otherwise, employers run the risk of losing their employees' motivation, or never getting it in the first place.

Charles Schwab once said, "I consider my ability to arouse enthusiasm among men the greatest asset I possess. The way to develop the best that is in a man is by appreciation and encouragement." I couldn't agree more, which is why I feel it is necessary to address this important part of our culture.

Of the 8,765 hours in a year, the average working American puts in 1,695 hours for "the man." That's about 19 percent of your time. Sure, you may think you have 81 percent of your time left over, but with an average of 33 percent spent sleeping and another 2 percent in the bathroom, you have only 46 percent of those precious hours left for everything else you need or want to do. If you are a small-business manager, a poll done by Staples shows that for you it's even worse. Not only do you clock in at the office or shop or studio or wherever your work takes you, but much of the precious time you have away from the workplace is spent on business affairs as well: even while driving, using the restroom, or spending time with your family. And in today's economy, where smaller staffs require workers to be more and more productive, the statistics are probably similar for just about everyone who has a job these days, management or not.

Since work takes up so much of our lives, it's vitally important that we not only find satisfaction in the job itself but in the appreciation we receive from coworkers and superiors for a job well done. At least, that's the hope.

LOVE WHAT YOU DO, DO WHAT YOU LOVE

Finding a job in this day and age is difficult. Finding a job that is satisfying—almost impossible. Until I was about twenty-six years old, my goals all centered on becoming a career woman. I wanted to have babies at some point, but I thought that being a card-carrying member of the professional world would be the best way to feel intelligent and valued and important to society.

With that in mind, I worked hard to make honors in graduate school, and even harder when it came time to start searching for "the perfect job." I wanted what Confucius talked about: "Choose a job you love and you will never have to work a day in your life." I got lucky when a spot opened up at Miami Children's Hospital, since I would be working with both inpatients and outpatients—exactly the location, specialty, and variety I was looking for.

Unfortunately, though, I soon found myself bored and searching for more. Going into it, I knew I was applying for a means to an income. Selfishly, though, I also wanted perfection. I loved the patient interaction and coworker friendships (even the rum cake we had each month in celebration of birthdays), but I soon learned that physical therapy wasn't always about helping people. It was just as much about piles of paperwork—boring paperwork. Day after day, I fought the urge to not get out of bed in the morning, and most likely still would be doing so today just to fulfill my obligations and continue to pay off my hefty student loans.

But after my experience on *The Bachelor* and seeing how much fun the people behind the scenes in TV land were having, I wanted what they had: to enjoy heading to work every day.

For a short time after the show wrapped, I returned to the hospital to pay the bills, but when the producers asked me to come back for seconds as the Bachelorette, I knew I had to take that leap of faith and satisfy my curiosity for life beyond the walls of the physical therapy department.

I put my PT license into "inactive" status and headed out to California thinking I was meant to be there—at least at that point in my life. It was scary. I had put so much time and effort and money into becoming a therapist and gave it all up with only the hope that Mike Fleiss could make ABC buy in to his idea of *The Bachelorette*. Until that happened and I signed on the dotted line months later, I dabbled in hosting and correspondent work, and I won't lie—I had an absolute blast.

But when I met Ryan Sutter, my focus changed again. It soon became all about being with him and the life we were hoping to create together. Luckily (and I mean *really* luckily), the paycheck that came after we agreed to televise our wedding allowed us to start our lives with a bank account that wouldn't require my returning to the daily grind I had known in Florida.

Every so often, I felt a twinge of regret about not following through with what I had so fervently educated myself in and not continuing to try to make a difference in the lives of my pediatric patients. Those regrets didn't last long. Once I was blessed with children of my own, I realized that what I truly wanted was what I had fought against for as long as I could remember: to be a stay-at-home mom.

Since I was a child, I had wanted to follow in my mom's footsteps—get a good education, provide for myself, and even get dressed up in business attire to head to work every day. I thought it was enlightened and admirable. I was so opposed to old-fashioned feminine stereotypes, I even ended a relationship on the verge of engagement because I thought my boyfriend saw me only as a baby breeder and homemaker. I felt that would make me seem inferior and unsophisticated.

With age and a lot of time spent getting to know the real me, I now find those roles to be incredible opportunities as well as surprisingly powerful. I may have lost a little mental acuity to the fog of mommy brain, but my clueless brain, as I call it, still knows what's important, and I don't think there is a more important job on the planet than raising a couple members of our next generation.

That's not to say that I look down on people with children who need to or decide to spend their workdays behind a desk, in front of a microphone, serving drinks, or in an apron or military fatigues. Everyone's gotta do what everyone's gotta do and I have mad respect for all the parents out there who work their tails off to support their families. The challenge for everyone, though, is finding something to devote your time to that is beneficial not only to your family's bank account, but also to your personal passion account.

My advice: Keep evolving and keep searching for contentment. Years and experience may change you, so be ready. As you grow, establish new goals and embrace new paths. I didn't reach the gateway to my present occupational path until I was thirty-four years old. And who knows: it may not even be my final professional path. I'm ready for it, though—ready to create a happy (work) place wherever life may take me.

WORKING HARD THROUGH HARD TIMES

For many, appreciation for the time you put in at work doesn't come easy, or fast, or maybe even ever. But for some of the self-proclaimed lucky ones, they recognize at some point on their timeline the true gift of just being employed, even if it's far from a dream job and it's bursting with challenges. Instead, they realize, that job keeps food on the table, a roof over their heads, a sense of security, and that job has either changed or saved their lives.

It took my friend Janet years, but after suffering devastating losses, she finally realized the beauty of her job and the role it played in helping her find her inner smile again. As the grand-daughter of a wealthy businessman in the banking and oil industry, she grew up not wanting for anything. For the first half of her life, she lived in the true lap of luxury, with multiple homes and private jets and extravagant, spontaneous trips to wherever her heart desired. Then she met John. John had moved to Janet's hometown of Borger, Texas, for an internship that he hoped would take him to Florida. Instead, he ended up on Florida *Street* and was introduced to Janet the night he arrived.

Janet fell in love instantly. Having dreamed of her Prince Charming riding into Borger on a white horse, she knew it was a sign when he drove into town in a white Ford Pinto. (Close enough, right?) As John was adamant about staying single, his feelings took much longer to develop. But once they did, they never faltered.

Shortly after Janet and John were married, they began their journey to parenthood, eventually welcoming four healthy children into the world. Without the ability to sustain the life-style she had always known after her parents lost their fortune, they relied on the income from John's civil engineering job and turned Janet's craft and painting hobbies into a budding art business that allowed her to be a stay-at-home mom. They named the business Happy Everything, because in her words, they "felt

so blessed." To this day, she still proudly creates personalized or-
naments, growth charts, journals, keepsake boxes, stained-glass
windows, trunks, canvases, step stools, and even pumpkins—
each decorated by hand. All she needs is a general idea and her
paintbrushes take over. She once told me, "I enjoy every second,"
even if she's under a deadline or the task at hand is difficult.

Besides her being a mother, wife, and Christian (not necessarily in that order), Janet's art is her calling. She realized that
it was much more than just a job after March 3, 2001—the
day her entire universe was forever changed.

On her first real date, their youngest daughter, Lynley, was
involved in a fatal car accident. Along with the boy who took
her to the movies that afternoon, she was pronounced dead on
the scene. She was sixteen. Three days later, Janet and John's
beautiful daughter was laid to rest.

After the service, their home was filled with those wishing
to express their condolences. With forty friends and loved
ones crammed in her workroom, Janet did what she had to
do to escape the reality that she would never see her daughter again—she completed an order for Happy Everything.

For years she continued to avoid reality through her work,
though the name of her business haunted her. She never wanted
to see the words again. Thankfully, one of her daughter's best
friends convinced her that Lynley would've wanted her to stand
by "Happy Everything" and continue doing what she loved. In
addition to her loving husband and children, caring friends,
and an unending faith, she survived the overwhelming heartache through her peaceful diversion of painting and learned to
keep a smile on her face—no matter what.

Compared with the loss of a child, it may sound like a relatively minor circumstance, but seven years later, they were

dealt further misfortune when John was let go from his job. Janet continued to paint, but her Happy Everything earnings weren't even close to the salary John had brought home. He searched for a job, but for an overqualified fifty-eight-year-old, the task proved impossible for many years. They had savings and retirement money stashed away, but through a rash of bad investments and significant debt, they burned through that and had to declare bankruptcy.

And it got worse—three substantial blows worse.

The first involved giving up the lifetime of memories attached to their large home and moving into a garage. The second: At fifty-nine, John took a job that required twelve-hour shifts walking the perimeter of a hotel in Colorado on freezing winter nights to ensure that the grounds were secure. The third and final blow came when they had to make a trip to a local pawnshop to sell what had represented their love and marital commitment for the past thirty-five years: their wedding rings.

As someone who truly cherishes what my engagement ring and wedding band signify, I can't imagine their sadness at saying good-bye to these precious tokens. Yes, they are only objects, but when you've worn something as a representation of the love you have for another person day and night for the better part of your life, it has to hurt down deep when you are forced to pawn them for cash.

Through it all, though, Janet put her whole self into doing what she loved—including painting—and her smile still prevailed. I can attest to that.

If my memory serves me right, I first encountered her bubbly personality in 2009. I had known of her and her business since the birth of my son in 2007 after we received a gorgeous stained-glass window she created for him, but we didn't officially meet until a couple years later. I've hired her to make special gifts and paint faces at children's birthday parties, celebrated baby showers and holidays together, and sat with her in my living room, trying to come up with a plan to light a fire under Happy Everything and get her back in the black. I knew, to a degree, of her and John's financial setbacks, but I didn't fully understand the extent.

Her beaming smile had hidden it all.

I don't know that I will ever have the pleasure of meeting anyone else quite like Janet. Over the course of her life, she's experienced tremendous highs, as well as the lowest of lows. She poured her life into her work to seek solace from pain, and through that work her pain was healed, and continues to be. Her business is now thriving, and I have no doubt that it is just the beginning of even greater success. She loves what she does and is grateful for the opportunity.

That, right there, is a recipe for Happy Everything.

HAPPY WORKERS ARE HARD WORKERS

Why do people leave their jobs? If you think it's because they want to make more money, you're wrong. If you think it's because they want a career change, wrong again. If you think it's because they won the lottery, nope, not even close. The number-one reason people leave their jobs, according to a Gallup poll of over 1 million American workers, is a bad boss. The study found that employees essentially quit their bosses, not their jobs—and all because of the way they feel they were treated.

Are you surprised? Or do you agree so much that you are one of the 2 million people who, according to Alan Hall in

Forbes magazine, quit their jobs each month even in our poor economic climate because they didn't like their boss?

Two million people every month! It seems to me that number would be much, much lower if workers were made to feel like happy contributors instead of stepped-on drones. Too many managers withhold their appreciation until it's time for Christmas bonuses or end-of-the-year reviews instead of handing it out regularly.

So if you assume your employees are there only for a paycheck, start thinking—and start thanking. And if you need a little inspiration, pick up a copy of Charles Dickens's classic tale *A Christmas Carol*. If you somehow missed this one in your high school English class, or when any number of cinematic versions show up on TV during December, from the classic Alastair Sim black-and-white film to the animated Mr. Magoo to the Muppets, the gist is this: the wealthy main character, Ebenezer Scrooge, finally awakens to the spirit of generosity and giving by the three ghosts of Christmas Past, Present, and Future. He ends his reign as a thank-you miser and showers his employee Bob Cratchit and his family not only with money but with credit and praise.

If you're a manager or executive, start expressing your gratitude to your staff on a regular basis, and just as Scrooge experienced, you will notice a difference not only in them but in yourself as well.

And this advice doesn't pertain only to those who toil away in an office. Whether or not you have a traditional nine-to-five job, we all work with people and for people. Do you employ a babysitter? A plumber? Do you ever visit the doctor for a checkup or the hair salon for a trim? Showing appreciation to all of the people who keep our lives running smoothly not only creates pride and positivity, but promotes better on-the-job performance as well.

Now, who could use a pat on the back?

FRIENDS AT WORK

I've had lots of jobs in my life. My parents, in an attempt to teach me the importance of financial independence and a strong work ethic, encouraged me to start earning my own spending money at an early age. I mowed our lawn, washed cars, did chores at home, and worked as a babysitter in our neighborhood. When I was sixteen, I got my first "real" job, making iron-on T-shirts and running the cash register at a little shop in Chesterfield Mall called T-Shirts Plus. From there I went on to help people find the perfect bathing suit or skateboard at a store named Splash, organize restaurant seating as a hostess, watch over swimmers as a lifeguard, wait tables, file paperwork, answer phones, submit insurance claims, sell gym memberships, and start a career in physical therapy. I loved the feeling of paying off my bills through hard work and, after graduate school, actually earning a living.

One of my favorite jobs had little to do with the minimal amount I was paid, and everything to do with fun and friends and the opportunity to indulge one of my passions: dancing. It took three years of persistent auditioning to finally earn a spot as a Miami Heat dancer. Once I made it, the other girls and I became fast friends, especially a group of about six of us. We saw one another at least three or four times a week for rehearsals, during public appearances, and at about forty home games per season.

We bonded over our team, our love of dancing, and oddly enough, fake eyelashes. Required to wear a strip of MAC #2's for every performance, we moaned and groaned about putting them on—well, at least I did. Even after taking training sessions with MAC makeup artists on how to properly apply them, I could never get it right.

Luckily, one of my closest friends on the squad was Ashley, the go-to lash applier. Practically every game, she would have to hustle from her full-time job as a social worker to the locker room at the American Airlines Arena to make herself up for game time. Even in a huge rush, she would always help me and usually anyone else who asked. Time was of the essence in the locker room but she didn't let that stop her from going out of her way to literally lend a hand to her friends, something I always appreciated with a squeeze and a thank-you after each application.

After Ashley and I hung up our red sequin tops, we remained close—not just as coworkers who bonded over false eyelashes, but as two dance lovers who had established a true friendship outside of work. We palled around on the weekends, sung "Happy Birthday" to each other wherever we happened to be celebrating that year, dressed up side by side on Halloween, attended each other's bachelorette parties, and witnessed each other walk down the aisle toward the loves of our lives. We met at work, but our friendship didn't stay at work. She was the kind of friend I hoped to find in that job. I just wish she could've stayed my friend for a lot longer.

On April 6, 2006, a pregnant Mary Ashley Clements was involved in a horrific car accident. Neither she nor her unborn child survived. I'll never get to tell her again how much I appreciated her presence in my life or her help with the little things, but every time I put on lashes or see her picture, I will always remember her unconditional kindness and genuine friendship.

If you feel as lucky as I do, you have met people through your job who make the day fly by, allow you to vent about things your family may not understand, help you finish a special project or celebrate life victories, and even meet you for a drink (or three) after a super-stressful day. Work, and the responsibilities that go with it, aren't always easy (including applying fake lashes), but no matter how big or small their contributions to your daily happiness, the people we work with can be the spoonful of sugar that makes the medicine go down.

The Research Proves It

Common sense tells us that we work better when someone tells us we're doing a great job. It's not just an instinct of parenting or a trick teachers use to encourage their students— science backs it up. If you don't believe me, or even your own mom, believe professionals like Jane Dutton. A leader in the positive psychology movement, she is based at the University of Michigan and believes that even the simplest gestures that show you care can add a level of humanity to a workplace— and raise performance levels.

A survey done by the American Psychological Association reported similar findings. After questioning more than 1,700 employees, researchers found that 93 percent are motivated to do their best work when they feel they are valued by their employers.

And these aren't the only findings out there. In 2009, researchers at the University of Pennsylvania's Wharton School did a study on positive behavioral effects of gratitude through a fund-raising experiment. Two groups were created. The first worked exactly as they always had, making calls to ask alumni for donations. The second group was given a pep talk in which the director told them she was very grateful for the wonderful work they were doing before they started making their calls.

Who do you think did a better job? That's right. The second group made 50 percent more calls over the week than group one, which significantly increased their odds of raising money for their school. Because the volunteers felt valued, they were far more eager to make their director proud.

As one blogger at the *Harvard Business Review* said, "There is far too little praise and appreciation in most work environments." And it's not just bosses and their staff who have this problem. Coworkers are just as guilty. So make it a point to appreciate a coworker's efforts this week. Notice the smile or the resultant improvement in their mood. Be proud of that, along with knowing that you are helping the company you work for through scientifically supported facts.

Passing on a little sunshine can never hurt, even if it's for the benefit of someone or something other than yourself. William Makepeace Thackeray, an English novelist, said it best: "Next to excellence is the appreciation of it."

A Teacher's Gift

Growing up, I always looked up to my aunt Nancy. She had studied fine arts overseas in Rome, and I admired her as a cultured and well-traveled artist—not to mention a fun-loving and beautiful one. The youngest of my mother's three sisters, she and her son, my cousin Courtney, lived with my mom and me for a few years—as did the papier-mâché Angel Gabriel she created during her time in Italy. Loaned to my mom to watch over me as a baby, it's an object I will never forget, something that made me feel safe and loved as a child even if I wasn't its creative inspiration. It was basically my intro to the arts, as well as to my aunt's talent.

Unfortunately, Nancy soon realized after her time in Rome that she didn't have the chops for the visual arts. What she does have the chops for is the literary arts—as demonstrated to our family every year when she and Courtney would write and illustrate stories as Christmas gifts. She has a wonderful way with words and a passion for storytelling, and my hope is that someday she'll write her own book filled with her inspirational messages. Here is just one of many. . . .

Going to school was hard work, and it always felt like a job. At St. Boniface Catholic Grade School, the bosses came in many forms, uniforms and titles. They included the black-gowned priests whom we called "Father," the brown-habited nuns whom we called "Sister," and lay teachers in suits or dresses whom we called Mr. or Mrs.

It was the weekend before Labor Day 1961, and I was about to start 5th grade, and for the 5th year in a row, I was not looking forward to once again being branded as a "remedial reader." Reading had never come easy to me, and I had learned that words were to be feared. Many a day and night I sat on my father's lap, book in hand, and I'd feel his arms tighten around me as I got the teeny tiny words wrong, time and time again.

From the first grade up to this doom-felt beginning of the 5th grade, I would brace myself for the reading tests. The nuns in their brown Franciscan cloaks with rulers in their hands would have each student read a paragraph and decide if they were an "advanced," "sufficient," or "remedial" reader. I will always remember the sound of the ruler as the nun smacked it into her palm when I either hesitated or mispronounced a word. You might as well have slapped me across my face—the humiliation was just as de-humanizing.

With every attempt, I got used to the laughter coming from my fellow classmates as I struggled through my assigned paragraph. I was grateful for the occasional rescue whispered by a helpful student sitting behind me, until I realized it could be used to cause me more embarrassment. One year, there was a passage that had the word "applause." I stopped cold. I heard "applesauce" and spoke it out loud. All the students roared—no one as loudly as my teacher.

After school, I would run home, retreat to the upstairs bathroom, lock the door, sit on the floor, and look into the bathroom's crystal doorknob to find my friend "Mary Jane" looking back at me from one of the facets. She was the one person I could trust to listen to and soothe my heart. When I told her my stories, she never stopped or chastised me for getting words wrong. She laughed along with my laughter but never laughed AT me, and she cried when I cried. She would repeat along with me: "I AM OK."

So those were the memories that were whirling through my brain on the eve of 5th grade. When we arrived at St. Boniface on the first day of school, we found out that the 5th and 6th grades would be divided into two. Half of each grade would be placed together and have its own teacher. My teacher was to be Mrs. Ida Smith. I do not remember the name of the other teacher, but it was a Mister (a young married man and an oddity never before seen within those hallowed walls). Because it seemed that all the cool kids were assigned to his class, I remember wanting him to be my teacher.

To this day, I remind myself that not getting what you want can actually be a wonderful stroke of luck.

In an effort to set the tone for the year, Mrs. Smith's first lecture was about those tiny bumps that sometimes appear for no reason in your mouth. She said that when you lied, they would appear, and she asked us never to lie to her. If she thought you were lying, she would ask you to open your mouth. To this day, when I get one of those tiny bumps, I question my integrity.

After another horrific reading test, Mrs. Smith asked me to stay inside during recess. My heart dropped. I wondered what new punishment was going to befall me now. She came and sat in the desk right in front of me, just me and her in the classroom. She took my small white hands inside her soft brown hands and our dark eyes connected. I started to well up with big puddles of tears until I heard her say, "You are not stupid." She told me to repeat after her: "I am not stupid." She then asked me: "Are you stupid?" and reminded me about those tiny bumps. I sat up straight, and said: "No, I AM NOT STUPID!" and immediately, my tongue made a 360 degree sweep to see if any tiny bumps appeared. Mrs. Smith asked to see inside and said, "It must be true . . . You are smart!"

I felt lighter than ever before.

I felt I had grown wings.

With just four simple but powerful words, Nancy felt valued as a student. With the encouragement of her "boss," she believed in herself and her abilities for the first time. She told me that that day she was taught that words and people are not to be feared. Instead, they could be her best friends and together they could write and tell their stories, "connecting one heart to another through lives and encounters and forever moments."

Nancy never got to show Mrs. Smith how high she flew or thank her for giving her such a life-changing gift. Her impactful legacy, though, lives on through my aunt Nancy and the lives she touches through her love of words.

So, to all the Mrs. Smiths out there who know the importance of a job well done—thank you. Thank you for caring enough to go the extra mile at work and lovingly plant seeds of confidence in the children of the world. Your words of inspiration not only give them the wherewithal to truly succeed as students, but positively influence their futures, allowing them to flourish as successful, productive, and compassionate adults.

HAPPILY EVER ACTIONS

~ Give yourself a break. Whether you schedule it as part of your day or it's just one of those days when it seems like nothing is going your way, excuse yourself, escape to a quiet corner, stay put, close your eyes, and in your private space, focus on the basics—breathing in through your nose and out through your mouth. Give yourself a good thirty seconds to visualize the perfect day and then get back at it.

~ You may not feel like it when you are dealing with your colleagues at work, but as the author Tony Gaskins said, "You teach people how to treat you by what you allow, what you stop, and what you reinforce." In behavioral psychology, it's called the "Law of Effect"—events that follow an action will weaken or strengthen the likelihood it will occur again. If you allow being overworked without additional compensation, you get overworked without compensation. If you blow off praise without genuine appreciation, chances are that you'll blow off the hope of future praise. It's your boss's responsibility to give you feedback on your productivity and outcomes, but it's your responsibility to make sure that he or she continues to do so, in the best way possible.

≈ If you are stuck in a job full of negative energy, don't let it overflow into your home life. Once you leave the "office," unburden your mind of any drama by meditating, writing down your struggles and throwing them out, or physically regrouping through walking or stretching, before you get home. Your home is meant to be your sanctuary. Keep it sacred.

≈ If you are stuck in a profession where you can't see eye to eye with the people you face day to day, or you are just plain unhappy, try to channel the late comedian George Burns, who once said, "I'd rather be a failure at something I love than a success at something I hate." Put effort into pushing the occupational clouds out of the way so that your dream job can be revealed. Ask yourself what you regret not pursuing—what you always thought about doing but were too afraid to fail—and write it down. If you do that, you will have taken the first necessary step toward making it a reality. Now keep going, one foot after the other, at whatever pace you can handle, and I have no doubt you'll get there.

Before I had kids, I worked in direct sales for a company called B's Purses. I did home parties where ladies could customize their own handbag, tote, or clutch. I learned the ropes from my sorority sister Angela, who was not only the sister of the founder but the rep with the most success. As new reps joined and worked "under" me, I took all her tips and tricks and passed them on, hoping to also pass on the success that Angela had helped me achieve. Yes, I earned a small percentage from their sales, but it wasn't about the extra bit of money. We were all part of a team and didn't let competition get the best of us. Instead, we focused on helping each other—offering up advice and assistance and celebrating one another's victories through encouragement and mentorship. It was a great job because we made it great, and you have the ability to do the same. Create an enjoyable work environment through the choices you make and the support you give, and you can make your job great too.

We Are All Connected

The life I touch for good or ill will touch
another life, and that in turn another,
until who knows where the trembling stops
or in what far place my touch will be felt.

—FREDERICK BUECHNER

CHAPTER EIGHT

THE WEB OF CONNECTIONS WE ALL WEAVE IS TANGLED with causes and effects. Whether direct or indirect, known or unknown, our links to others can drastically influence the path people choose for their lives, the attitudes they embrace, and the actions they take as they face their future.

We all live in our own little sections of the world, but each of us has the power to reach beyond our own borders and touch other lives, no matter how far away. A study published in the *Proceedings of the National Academy of Science* confirms it. The researchers found that if someone behaves generously, up to three degrees of others feel inspired to spread that altruistic spirit at a later date, to different people. That means one person can inspire generosity in three people, and those three people can inspire it in nine people, and those nine people can inspire it in twenty-seven, and so on and on. We can't control all the ripples caused by our pebble's effect on the world's body of water, but we know they're there, even if the pebble fell so softly that the ripples can't be seen.

Moving forward, think of the effect you have on the world and its effect on you. We are all touched by others. We all have the power to connect and the power to affect. It's up to you to use that power wisely.

Grace Under Fire

Each year, Americans give about $300 billion to charitable causes in hopes of effecting positive change, whether in their community or on the far side of the world. However, there aren't any statistics for the countless lives that have been altered by kind words, a gentle touch, a listening ear, a random act of kindness, a beautiful vision, or a fearless deed of generosity. We do know that they happen, though.

StoryCorps (StoryCorps.org), a national radio documentary project that has archived more than 40,000 stories of American individuals, recorded one of my favorite examples of an extraordinary gesture of goodwill. It's the story of a social worker named Julio Diaz.

In 2008, Diaz was riding the subway on his way home to the Bronx from work, planning to stop at his regular diner for dinner. His plans were drastically changed when a teenager sprang out at him, pulled a knife, and demanded that Diaz hand over his money.

Diaz watched as the teen walked away with his wallet. Instead of thanking his lucky stars that he wasn't physically injured, Diaz did something that would never cross most of our minds—he called out to his assailant, "Hey, wait a minute. You forgot something. If you're going to be robbing people for the rest of the night, you might as well take my coat to keep you warm."

Then he did something even more unimaginable: he invited the young man to join him for dinner. A warm coat, and now a hot meal? The stunned boy agreed. At the restaurant, the teen noted how friendly his victim was to everyone who worked there, from the waitress to the dishwasher.

He asked Diaz if he owned the restaurant.

"No," Diaz said.

"Then why are you so nice to everyone?"

"That's how I was raised."

The boy was shocked, thinking, *People actually live like that?*

The bill came, but the teen still had the stolen wallet. Surprisingly, he returned it, and Diaz kept his promise to pay for dinner. He then handed his mugger twenty dollars. Following Diaz's lead, the teen handed over his knife. Hopefully, he never used one in a potentially violent situation again.

To me, this story is a poignant illustration of what Benjamin Disraeli, a British prime minister, once said: "The greatest good you can do for another is not just to share your riches but to reveal to him his own."

Julio Diaz made a conscious and brave decision to lend a hand and impart an important life lesson to someone who could've easily killed him that day. He chose kindness toward a stranger over fear and self-preservation. I don't know that I could be as courageous or as trusting in someone who took advantage of me in such a frightening way, but I will remember the message of this inspiring story and attempt to follow its noble example.

JOINED AT THE SOCIAL HIP

Whether in the media or my blogs, social media posts, or this book, I've always been open to sharing my battles and victories with anyone interested to know them. It's my way of both shouting my happy moments from the rooftops and also letting those who may be experiencing similar battles know that they aren't alone and that they shouldn't give up hope. The story of my and Ryan's difficulties in getting pregnant is no different.

During that time, I got letters not only from friends but also from people I had never met who wished me well and thanked me for sharing my story—something many in the public eye are understandably hesitant to do for fear of judgment or to maintain some semblance of privacy. Hearing that someone else in the universe was experiencing a struggle like theirs gave them the inspiration to keep fighting and make their own baby dreams come true. I can't put into words how much these connections touched my heart, but something Herman Melville once said comes pretty close: "We cannot live only for ourselves. A thousand fibers connect us with our fellow men; and among those fibers, as sympathetic threads, our actions run as causes, and they come back to us as effects."

Now, in our age of social media, we are connected like never before. At a moment's notice, we can catch up with what just about anyone in the world is up to or reach out to them via their website, blog, Twitter page, or Facebook wall. I use the gift of this generation's technological advances to interact with people from all over the world. I don't have an assistant who poses as me online. I respond personally to specific questions or interesting comments while snuggling with my Disney Junior–loving kids, on road trips (as a passenger, of course), or during any other moment I can bury my face in my phone. The best part: I almost always get a thank-you in return.

This medium and its ability to allow us to connect to those we've never met has also given me cherished gifts. Take, for example, this Facebook message I received back in October 2009. Cheryl Church wrote,

How wonderful to name your daughter Blakesley!!! I work at Purdue and had the pleasure of watching your grandparents walk through campus every day holding hands. Now that they have moved to assisted living, I miss seeing them. They have to be thrilled with your choice of name. Your grandparents showed everyone here what love was all about. How proud you must be of them . . . and your children. God bless you all.

I responded with a message of deep thanks for letting me in on something so touching and beautiful. I certainly was incredibly proud of my grandparents and the legacy of love they have created (which was a big reason we chose them to be our daughter's namesake). I still am and always will be. Without technology, I most likely would never have heard her story or been given such a moving tribute to my heritage. That's just another reason that (as my husband says) I'm addicted to my computer.

Even though we may never have lunch with Twitter followers, Facebook friends, or visitors to our blogs or websites, we can still share information and stories, as well as ask questions and get answers from those with shared experiences. We can enlighten a person's day, get help with a frustrating issue, or offer a sympathetic hand to someone experiencing a hard time. Thanks to social media, we can do all that and more.

SECOND CHANCES

There have been times in my life when I connected with someone the moment we were first introduced. Jennifer Carter is one of those people.

One day in 2006, when Ryan and I had tried what felt like everything short of in-vitro fertilization, I received a call from a friendly voice. Jen introduced herself, explaining that she worked for a company that had patented a device called the OV-Watch, and said that after hearing of our struggles, she thought it could help us achieve our dream of becoming parents. Not only did OV-Watch end up playing a key role in educating me on my prime ovulation days, which ultimately facilitated my journey to pregnancy, but I also gained a close friend. And the connection had even greater implications down the road.

Let me explain.

In 2009, Jen heard through the media grapevine that television host Giuliana Rancic and her husband, Bill, the first winner of *The Apprentice,* were experiencing difficulties conceiving a baby. Just as she had done with me, she wanted to send Giuliana an OV-Watch in the hopes that it would help the Rancics achieve their dreams of welcoming a child of their own into the world. One problem: Getting in touch with a media personality is not necessarily the easiest thing. So Jen reached out to me in hopes that I may have met Giuliana or have information about how she could get in touch. Luckily, I had had the pleasure of meeting both Rancics and attempted to make an introduction.

I'm not sure whether Jen was ever able to connect with Giuliana and Bill and if they ever tried using OV-Watch, but from the moment Jen became aware of their struggles, she was drawn to their story and followed it closely in the press. Along with millions of others, Jen found out on October 18, 2011, that Giuliana was dealing with an even more ominous obstacle: breast cancer.

Jen remembers reading that Giuliana's gynecologist had found a lump but that it was deemed "no big deal." In reality, that lump turned out to be a very big deal. Thankfully, though, her fertility specialist's stern orders helped find it early enough.

Before he would start their third round of in-vitro fertilization, he insisted that Giuliana get a mammogram and ultrasound. She reluctantly carried out his requests and was given life-altering news: cancer.

When Jen heard, it struck a chord with her. A very scary chord.

Not six months earlier, during a routine exam, Jen also had been told by her ob-gyn that she had what was likely a harmless cyst in her breast. After hearing Giuliana's story, though, she decided to disregard her doctor's nonchalance and made an appointment to get a mammogram the very next day. Just as Giuliana had experienced, Jen's radiologist told her that the lump they were investigating was "not a cyst," and soon she was scheduled for a lumpectomy. In Giuliana's case, the doctors knew the mass that showed up on the screen was cancer, so her initial lumpectomy was a necessary procedure in attempting to save her life. In Jen's case, they knew it wasn't a fluid-filled cyst, but they were unsure whether it was a benign fibroadenoma or a malignant growth. A simple biopsy was too risky. Only surgery could tell.

So she waited for a surgery date. And while she waited, she worried. She was fearful that the similarities between her story and Giuliana's would continue and a cancer diagnosis would be in her near future as well. She thought of her husband and her kids and how her once-upon-a-time dreams had played out over the course of her life. Was she proud of her accomplishments or regretful of her choices?

This is what she told me:

All my life I've wanted to be a mother, and I've spent years helping other women accomplish their own maternal dreams. I pictured my life as a mommy—easy and carefree. We'd bake cookies, skip through fields of daisies, and I'd never raise my voice. I was naive. I had no idea how hard life is when you're a Mom.

My children are eight and six now, and although I try very hard to be the mother I planned to be—I'm not. My commitment and obligation to my career and our financial stability as a family has been, unfortunately, my first priority over the last eight years. I'm gone most mornings when they are getting ready for school, and if I get to put them to bed and read my little girl a bedtime story, I'm rushing to finish it so that I can handle the rest of my life before midnight.

Every single day I promise myself that I will calm my life down and try to be a more attentive, kinder, more loving mother. Some days I am able to accomplish it and some days I just don't live up to my own expectations.

Already feeling like a terrible mother and never putting my kids first, I then added the thought of a breast cancer diagnosis and ended up having a few very dramatic breakdowns. Since hearing Giuliana's nearly parallel story and getting myself checked, I was not only convinced that I was going to die, but I also feared that my children would never know the mother that I so wanted to be.

However, I am excited to tell you that my lump was benign and I will be fine! I now have a second chance to be the mother that I know my children deserve.

And I know she will be. For this already incredibly thoughtful person, I know this brush with dread will alter her life's trajectory, and that of her family.

Without the fear of following in Giuliana's footsteps and receiving a cancer diagnosis, Jen wouldn't have analyzed her own past and tried to change her future. It was a much-needed cue to move her sweet children up the totem pole of priorities. And all of this happened thanks to the honesty and bravery of Giuliana Rancic, a woman Jen now considers a hero, and to whom she feels forever connected, even if it's from afar.

KEEP YOUR EYES AND EARS OPEN

Reminders to enjoy life come in many shapes and sizes. In our fast-paced society, we're often too busy or preoccupied to notice them, but if we are lucky, they continue to seek us out and eventually we get the message.

I remember one day in particular that I was living the rush. I was at the Los Angeles International airport and, along with what seemed like thousands of other people, I was caught up in the stress of traveling. In a moment of calm, I scanned the room, curious about the other people at my gate. Interestingly, I was not drawn to a frustrated traveler in a heated conversation with an airline representative or a mother trying to corral her little ones to take a potty break, but instead to an airport rarity: sitting across from me was a middle-aged woman with long, curly black hair and glasses, peacefully sitting still. She wasn't reading or writing or talking or tweeting or racing to get on a plane. She was merely taking it all in, a subtle smile lighting up her face.

I took her cue. I stopped what I was doing and chose to live the calm instead of the rush, at least for a few fleeting minutes. She was my angel of the day, reminding me to slow down, empty my mind, and just breathe.

Ever since, I try to picture her when I'm swallowed by the daily events that raise my blood pressure. I'm not always successful, but just visualizing the calm aura she exuded amid a sea of stress helps me decelerate when my pace is going dangerously fast.

My best friend from graduate school has a similar story. As a full-time physical therapist and mother of three girls under nine years old, she is always on the go. After an especially trying week, she was feeling out of control (and she's usually impressively in control).

She powered through her list for the day, including a quick trip to the grocery store while her girls were in school. There, she came across a woman in her midseventies she could've easily passed in her hurry to stay on schedule. But noticing that the woman needed help picking up a fallen bag of groceries, my friend decided to lend her a hand.

"Thank you!" the woman said. "Do you want to come home with me?"

My friend jokingly replied that that might be easier than returning to the chaos of her house.

The woman laughed and then said something my friend will never forget: "Just so you know, I really, really miss the chaos."

With those ten simple words, this complete stranger transformed the rest of my friend's day, week, and maybe even year . . . and most likely her family's too. She now actively attempts to enjoy the chaos. We all should.

THANKS IN GIVING

For my family, charity work is our way to give back. We feel lucky for all our blessings, so whether it's through time or money or posing in our birthday suits for a local fund raiser called the Vail Undressed calendar (covered up in all the right places, of course), we try to share that luck and love with organizations we feel connected to, even if it's for people we've never had the pleasure of meeting.

In 2008, we were given a wonderful opportunity to pay it forward. As part of an agreement we made with Skechers for an ad campaign titled "Nothing Compares to Family," the company would donate $5,000 to the charity of our choosing. After working in a children's hospital for four years and seeing firsthand the hardships thrust upon those with babies in the cardiac and neonatal units, as well as going through it to a lesser degree ourselves, I felt particularly passionate about helping out a Vail family dealing with a heavy load. I had heard about them through a friend at the Vail Valley Charitable Fund, a corporation formed in 1996 to help people in our community facing critical medical emergencies.

Even though it wasn't our money to give, we felt honored to be given a choice in where the donation would end up. Skechers easily could have donated to the many organizations they support, but instead they allowed us to help a local family through their blind generosity.

Not knowing this family personally, we hoped that the money would lessen their financial burden a bit. On December 4, 2008, I received a Facebook message that let me know it had done just that (I've changed the name to protect the recipient's privacy). It said:

> Hi! I am Mary Smith. I am writing to thank you and Skechers for the grant you made possible through the Vail Valley Charitable Foundation. My family was the recipient of it and I cannot thank you enough. I had a son born at 34 weeks and then my daughter was born 17 months later with a congenital

heart defect. The bills we have accumulated are immense and the grant from the foundation will help. I hope to send you a more personal note but I couldn't pass up this chance to say thank you. You have no idea how much this helps. Thank you, Mary Smith and family

So simple. So genuine. So cherished.

When I shared this message with my contact at Skechers, her response was: "I just got chills. How great to read and know that you touched someone's life in that way." The way I see it, Ryan and I were only a tiny part of their corporate kindness. I'm just thankful that we were any part at all.

THE TRUE MEASURE OF MY MAN

The seventeenth-century English clergyman Robert South once said, "If there be any truer measure of a man than by what he does, it must be by what he gives." I believe whole-heartedly in this message, but after watching what my husband accomplished in 2010, I would have to expand it to say: The truest measure of a man is not only in doing or giving but in uniting the two for a cause greater than his alone.

That summer, Ryan's task was the 10.10.10 challenge. The goal: get 10,000 people to donate $10 to a charity organization called First Descents in honor of the group's tenth anniversary. Founded by a longtime friend of ours named Brad Ludden, FD provides free outdoor adventure programs to eighteen- to thir-ty-nine-year-olds who are either battling or have survived can-cer. The $100,000 objective would allow one hundred young adults to attend and experience the inspirational power that Ryan and I have experienced firsthand.

Over the course of six months, Ryan competed in twelve races (although the list originally followed the theme and started with ten), including a twenty-four-hour mountain bike race, the New York City Marathon, the Lake Placid Ironman, and a 100-mile mountain bike race at altitudes as high as 12,424 feet. At the end of the challenge, it was estimated that Ryan had trained for over 700 hours, traveled more than 8,500 miles, and climbed the equivalent of Mount Everest four times. Yes, he's crazy, but crazy in the best way.

With the help of both individual and corporate donations, Ryan was able to achieve his goal, and First Descents was able to cover the program expenses for one hundred people looking to defy their disease, experience a new adventure, bond with empathetic new friends, and gain a newly invigorated strength of spirit to get back to their fight.

One of those participants was Laura Esposto. She hadn't heard of Ryan's challenge before she applied to the program, but it was people like her who made him attempt it in the first place.

Laura was diagnosed with chronic myeloid leukemia when she was just twenty-three years old. The day after Christmas 2008, the biggest battle of her life began as she started her first round of chemo. Never giving her full remission through her treatments, her doctors set out on a search for a bone marrow match in February 2010. It was the only remaining option for killing the disease that was slowly killing her.

Through a national search over several months, a match was found and her transplant was performed in Houston in August 2010. She returned home to Philadelphia after 100 days of isolation a "complete disaster." She told me that everything that made her who she was, was gone. Her body was destroyed, but even more so, her spirit was destroyed. Even with a very strong support system in a new husband, a mother who temporarily quit her job to be her full-time caregiver, and friends galore, she found herself in a severe state of depression. She realized she needed an escape and searched on young adult cancer forums for retreats that catered to her demographic. First Descents seemed like the perfect fit. Because she was unable to submerge herself in water due to the risk of infection, the kayaking and surfing options that she thought would come easily to her were both out. So she applied for a rock-climbing program that was way outside her comfort zone. Even though she was only seven and a half months post-transplant and still very weak, she was accepted, because at FD every young adult affected by cancer is eligible, regardless of physical challenges, diagnosis, or prognosis.

Feeling anxious and scared, she headed out to Estes Park, Colorado, early in 2011. A staffer nicknamed Remix picked her up at the airport in Denver and immediately got to work giving her a nickname. The group has found that it's not only a great way to break the ice, but it also bonds those involved in a new and exciting special "club." Most important, it gives everyone a way to leave everything behind—their names, their fears, and especially their disease. Nothing seemed to stick with Laura until she mentioned her childhood days as a Girl Scout. Since then she's been known, at least in the First Descents family, as "Cookie" (and fittingly, her husband, who attended an FDRock program for caregivers, is known as "Leche").

During her weeklong adventure, she discovered an entire community of people who weren't afraid of her or for her. She explained to me that meeting them was like looking in a mirror—they looked like her, had feelings like her, had dreams and goals like her, and had suffered all too similarly to her. They may not have all had the same diagnoses, but they all showed up with the same cracks in their spirit. Through the environment of safety at camp, they were able to be soul-deep honest and open and fill in those cracks together. In her words: "FD gave me a network of survivors and staff who could relate without pity." It connected her to a group of people she didn't know she was missing, a group she now would find it hard to live without. Through Ryan's challenge, she and ninety-nine others were able to attend programs of their choice and, through them, change their lives.

The chain of beneficial change didn't stop there. Laura, and others like her, wanted to give back to the organization that had given so much, so they joined Team First Descents, setting out to accomplish their own challenges in the name of their charitable mission. Laura began running and hasn't stopped, completing three 5K races and two half marathons with a fund-raising total so far of about $3,000. That's three more lives changed.

The list goes on and on, and actually includes me, our kids, and Ryan himself—all due to the efforts of his alter ego: G-String. On the day we were introduced to the workings of FD programs, Ryan was given that nickname after I received mine. Here's how it went down: A staffer nicknamed Woogie asked me if I had thought about what I'd like to be called. I hadn't prepared at all. (Bad call #1.) On the spot, I thought of my function in Ryan's challenge and decided I should go with something that represented support. I asked her, "Can you think of the name of a well-known cheerleader or big supporter?" (Bad call

#2.) Rephrased, I might have led her down a different path, but almost immediately and very enthusiastically, she said, "Jock Strap!" And since they considered us a team, he was called G-String. Forevermore, we will be known as undergarments. I guess it could have been worse, though—we could be known as what our undergarments support!

At the very least, our nicknames provide hysterical inter-actions with anyone who dares call out to us in public. For Ryan, his nickname also provided a way to separate his in-credibly humble self from the uncomfortable accolades that came with achieving his 10.10.10 challenge goal. He didn't ask to be recognized (he actually requested not to be), but in receiving the Golden Paddle award for raising the most money for First Descents that year, it was only fair that he properly thank his alter ego in a letter that he read aloud as his speech that night.

Dear G-String,

I wanted to write you in praise of your 10.10.10 challenge and thank you for the inspiration and opportunity it provided me to complete a challenge of my own. Though I have never had cancer, I feel as though, through you and Team First Descents, cancer has forever changed my life.

I knew when I took the challenge that, like you, my physical strength and conditioning would be tested. I knew it would be hard work. I accepted that and looked forward to the opportunity to seek the untapped fortitude of my will and spirit. I devised a focused plan and dove in headfirst.

We Are All Connected

My first events were tough. I was sore but it felt good to be active, to push myself beyond my perceived limits. Though tired, I felt strong. The inspiration of the Challenge motivated me. In some ways I felt unstoppable.

I had expected the workload and the effect it would have on my body. I was ready for the pain and the suffering. I was positive that I would emerge a better person. I began to expect it, actually. In fact, I began to believe that I was a better person. I felt great. I was fit. I was in the best shape of my life. People admired me for what I was doing. I believed I had found the ability to summon an incredible inner strength, to persevere. When I was not training or racing, I walked tall and with confidence. I was proud. So proud, in fact, that I neglected to see the effect the challenge was having on the rest of my life.

You should know that I am married and have two young children. I became so focused on the challenge that I neglected the rest of my life. I didn't notice the disappointment on my son's face when I turned down his offers to draw so that I could go out for a bike ride. My daughter's connection to me was just developing though I failed to notice the way she chased me around looking for a hug or a moment with her dad. I was too busy worrying about the next race or what I should be eating.

My wife, the woman who was picking up all the slack while I was out "becoming a better person," was the one whom I took for granted the most. When I wasn't training,

I was tired and of little help around the house. Because of
my physical efforts, I somehow felt privileged. I believed I
deserved to do whatever I wanted, whenever I wanted, with
whomever I wanted, regardless of the consequences or
the impact on my family. In my inspired effort to complete
the challenge, I was losing all the things most important to
me. Though it was love that originally inspired me, it was
love that was suffering the most. I did not want to admit it.
Though my focused eye could not see it, I knew in my heart
that I was not winning this challenge. I had lost sight of the
purpose. I had not grown at all from the ability to suffer
through physical pain. Though from the outside it was not
apparent, I was, in fact, a worse person. I broke down. I
truly lost it.

It was in that moment of despair that the challenge
changed for me. It was no longer about the training or the
races or the singular focus on purposefully torturing my
physical being. Certainly, I would still get the work done.
Quitting would have not solved anything. Rather than
riding a thoroughbred into each day, I would choose to
walk a turtle. I was going to treat my life as my kids had
tried to show me—with a true appreciation for the moment
(good or bad), and an attentive and inquisitive eye towards
anything really fun. No more suffering. Racing and training
would be fun. Work would be fun. Life would be fun.

Though perhaps the most significant hill to climb, I
would work to show my wife how much I appreciate her.
How much I knew she did for me. How sorry I was for
compromising her life and how much I truly loved her.

We Are All Connected

I had taken a lot from my acceptance of the challenge, when in the end it should have been more about giving.

Giving back to FD. They were and still are the source of my inspiration.

Giving back to my family. Without their support, I could not have done any of this.

Giving back to life. There are truly no guarantees. Each moment is a blessed opportunity and the choices we make within them will forever shape our destinies.

G-String: I am forever grateful for your willingness to accept such a mighty challenge. Your demonstration of the indomitable human will not only propelled me through the difficult physical challenges, it uncovered the existence of an equally powerful human spirit and the heart that seeks to guide us to places of unimaginable strength, should we simply choose to follow it.

I am forever in your debt.

Signed, *Ryan Sutter*

In giving of himself, he actually gained a better self. In the end, he became a better husband, a better father, a better son, and a more empathetic friend. He connected with hundreds if not thousands of others he would never personally know but whom he inspired all the same, and enhanced the connections with the people who know and love him the best.

I've always held my husband in the most sacred part of my heart, even before I knew him, but after living through the challenge with him, I saw the true measure of my man. And as long as he continues to embody the lessons he learned, it will forever be unmatched.

SERENDIPITOUS STRANGERS

As I alluded to in Chapter 6, in my opinion my aunt Nancy is the most talented writer in my family. Always a free spirit, she lived the life of a very successful corporate executive in the fashion industry, yet decided to throw caution to the wind at age fifty-two and apply for a job with the Peace Corps. Eighteen months later, less than one month shy of her fifty-fourth birthday, she was headed to Kenya. It was a wonderful adventure for her, in more ways than one, but until I can get her to write a book of her own, I wanted to share another one of her stories and what I believe to be a perfect demonstration of the lessons taught to us by complete strangers.

I have become accustomed to seeing groups of school children walking for miles, all in their school uniforms, to and from school every day. Some of the groups are made up of 10 kids or more, some are groups of 4 and occasionally I will see them 2 by 2—but I don't remember in rural Kenya ever seeing a single school child walking alone.

So I remember for just a second, that when I first caught sight of The Girl on Ngong Road, that seeing this young (probably about 7) school girl walking alone on the crowded streets and sidewalks of this busy Nairobi street, that it seemed out of place. She was walking slowly but determinedly about half a block ahead of me, her back pulled straight by a heavy book bag, head focused straight ahead, her hands swishing rhythmically over her navy blue school uniform skirt. If I found this an odd sight, it seemed that none of the hundreds of Kenyan pedestrians thought it was odd for a single, small school girl to be walking alone. They passed her by, her head at their thigh height, hardly noticing that they were doing a round-about around her. As I came up behind her and began my own round-about, we both, keeping our heads straight ahead, angled our eyes to take in this person passing by. In that instant, we both cracked a small smile.

As a *mzungu* (white person), I was used to seeing this slight smile when a Kenyan child made eye contact with me, because they could try out their high-pitched English "How are you?" But this little girl moved her eyes to their ever-forward position and went about her determined walk. The curb was coming up and people were stopped, so I could not finish my round-about around her. We slowed down but kept in step, occasionally angling our eyes to get another peek at each other. As the crowd started to cross the street, we moved forward. As we got to the curb, I stopped and noticed a car rounding the corner as the little girl started to step off the curb right into its path. I placed my hand on her shoulder and said "*simama*," stop. She looked up, smiled and suddenly took my hand.

I can still feel those fingers, soft and small, trusting this stranger. We waited until the coast was clear and then crossed the street. As we continued on our journey, she continued to hold my hand. In Kiswahili, I asked her name, and she told me it was "Rose." I told her that was a beautiful name and that my mother's name is Rosemary and my sister's name is Roseanne. She gave me a very big smile when I told her this—small connections to others seemed to bring her pure joy. She tried out her English, asking my name, and we continued our small encounter with small conversation. A man walked by, did a double take, and said hi to Rose. She introduced me to her uncle as *"rafiki yangu,"* my friend.

When we reached the huge intersection that connected Ngong Rd with three other large streets, it was time for us to part. I had to cross this six-lane road without the help of stop lights and Rose had to continue on her current path. I asked if she would be OK and said that it was nice to meet her. She smiled and squeezed my hand one more time and went back to her singular determined walk. I played dodge-car across this thoroughfare, holding my breath all the way. Once I was on the other side, I exhaled and glanced back across the street to see if I could see Rose. I had looked where I thought she would have been by now and did not see her, but then pulled my eyes back to the spot where we had parted and there she was, big smile and small hand waving as hard as she could. I had helped her not to walk in front of an oncoming car, and she had willed me safely across a treacherous intersection.

One good deed.

For the next five minutes, we kept walking together, just on opposite sides of the same street, and kept looking across, smiling and waving until we were too far apart to see each other. I don't know for how long that Rose will remember me, but I know I will never forget her, and I will never forget the feel of those small hands nestled in mine.

HAPPILY EVER ACTIONS

~ Usually my dad's e-mail forwards are politically based and don't survive the delete button for long. One day he sent me a message with the subject line: "photos to restore your faith in humanity." About halfway through the pictures, one of them stood out. Taped to a vending machine was a dollar bill in a plastic bag that said: "Your snack is on me! Enjoy your day ☺." I thought it was a sweet way to spread happiness, albeit in an anonymous way. Try it. I have, and I can tell you that the happiness I walked away with was worth much more than the $1.50 I left.

~ Remember that your story may not be your story alone. In sharing your struggle and the lessons you may have learned along the way, you open up the possibility of connection and action and transferred strength. You may not have a public forum as Giuliana Rancic did, but with a little thing called the World Wide Web and a whole new culture of bloggers, social media, and message boards, you can make an everlasting difference to just about anyone, regardless of where they are in the world.

~ Even if you don't feel you have a compelling story to share, don't think you aren't able to reach out and touch someone. Just as Martin Luther King Jr.

once said, "Everybody can be great . . . because anybody can serve. You don't have to have a college degree to serve. You don't have to make your subject and verb agree to serve. You only need a heart full of grace. A soul generated by love." We all are given the gift of time—even if we don't feel that we ever have enough, while here on earth. Research volunteer opportunities in your area through sites like DoSomething.org/volunteer or VolunteerMarch .org. Depending on your interests and passions, you may actually meet someone who will change your life, or vice versa.

Unexpected Blessings

I will love the light for it shows me the way,

yet I will endure the darkness because

it shows me the stars.

—OG MANDINO

WITHOUT A TIME MACHINE, THERE'S NO WAY TO KNOW what the changes we're experiencing now will lead to. I do, however, believe that everything has a purpose. As Marilyn Monroe once said, "I believe that everything happens for a reason. People change so that you can learn to let go, things go wrong so that you appreciate them when they're right, you believe lies so you eventually learn to trust no one but yourself, and sometimes good things fall apart so better things can fall together." Known for dealing with significant inner demons of her own, Marilyn's life on earth was not free from pain, and yet her words suggest that even she believed that there is a long-term deeper meaning to the events that occur in our lives.

A colleague recently told me that she once said, "Everything happens for a reason," to an acquaintance, and the lady defensively snapped back at her, "People who say that have clearly never had anything bad happen to them." The lady's reaction seemed to imply that, to her, anyone who bought into that sentiment assumed that those who are the victims of bad things somehow deserve it. I imagine she thinks that bad things just happen for no reason at all.

For me, and it seems the late Marilyn Monroe, the phrase "everything happens for a reason" suggests not that bad things happen as punishment but rather that there is a deeper purpose for all life's events, even if they are the most difficult thing we could ever conceive of experiencing or if their meaning is hidden from immediate comprehension.

That said, I understand that in some circumstances, accepting that there is a purpose to suffering a devastating loss can seem impossible, especially in the event that a life you have cherished has come to an end. As my friend Dana Weiss asked me, "How do you explain the death of a child?" When you're in the midst of grief, you can't. There is no explanation. There's just pain and anger and profound sadness.

However, I choose to believe that we are all part of a bigger picture and that death, or any other type of suffering, has meaning. Whether it is revealed right away or decades down the road, or remains obscure until our own dying day, it does exist and when you acknowledge that, you are doing anything but dishonoring those who have passed and the struggles you've survived. In fact, by rising back up toward the light of happiness, you are actually doing your part to honor those who suffered and give value to what happened.

I may be standing at the top of my life's mountains at this point in my timeline, but I've spent my share of time in its valleys, and wholeheartedly believing that everything happens for a reason has gotten me through each and every time. Whether I was experiencing depression or loss, betrayal or physical pain, believing that there is a reason for my hardships has always helped me over the hurdles. To survive the hurt, I had to believe that my darkest moments weren't all for naught. They couldn't have been.

As a self-proclaimed wimp who does not handle pain well, be it physical or emotional, I know from time to time I will falter from my goal of acknowledging the bigger picture. However, I do have a plan: to optimistically keep searching for meaning and gratitude and grace when I need them most. The bumps in the road teach us to be cautious the next time around, show us the depth of our courage and strength, and may even fling us forward onto a life path that we may not have otherwise chosen for ourselves: a path that is unexpectedly blessed.

It's All About Perspective

My husband recently told me that he wasn't a "glass-half-full kind of guy." He said, "I prefer to choose the right size glass so that it's always full."

My response: You don't always have the option to choose the size of your glass, but you do always have the option to choose how you view it.

As I've said throughout these pages, I attempt to look at life from an optimistic viewpoint ("attempt" being the keyword there). No matter what life throws at me, I do my best to look toward hope and a greater meaning bigger than myself. And according to two studies I found, if you do the same, you will be both more resilient and healthier.

In the first study, Dr. Dennis Charney, dean of Mount Sinai's School of Medicine, examined 750 remarkable Vietnam veterans. For six to eight years, each one of these brave men was a prisoner of war, kept in solitary confinement and tortured. Yet unlike fellow war vets who hadn't suffered such extreme treatment, they weren't weighed down by the common psychological consequences of depression or post-traumatic stress disorder. Charney wanted to know why they were so resilient. What he found is that the prisoners of war shared ten characteristics that allowed them to come out of their horrifying experiences without lasting mental injury. Included in these characteristics were social supports, humor, altruism, spirituality, the ability to face fears, being trained, and having a moral compass, a role model, and a mission in life. At the top of the list, though, was optimism.

In the second study, Christopher Peterson and his psychology colleagues at the University of Michigan found that, after studying ninety-nine graduates of Harvard University for thirty-five years, those who had a pessimistic style of describing life events at age twenty-five had significantly poorer health later on in adulthood than those with an optimistic outlook.

And if those results aren't enough to make you see the brighter light of optimism, maybe you'll listen to Martin Seligman. When asked to share the one piece of knowledge he would like everyone to know, the author, prolific researcher, and founder of positive psychology said, "If you are a pessimist in the sense that when bad things happen you think they are going to last forever and undermine everything you do, then you are about eight times as likely to get depressed, you are less likely to succeed at work, your personal relationships are more likely to break up, and you are likely to have a shorter and more illness-filled life. That's the main discovery I associate with my lifetime."

So, if you are ready to give yourself a better chance at living a healthy, happy, more successful life, join me in taking the bad with the good and weaving it together into the best.

A GOLDEN OPPORTUNITY IN A SILVER LINING

For much of America, when you hear the name Jenny Mc-Carthy, you think of a witty, candid blonde who is a devoted mother with a huge fan in Hugh Hefner, a successful career in the literary and television worlds, and a very public advocacy for autistic children around the globe. At least, that's what I think of.

I've long admired Jenny's humor, beauty, and zest for life from afar—especially after reading her best-selling books about motherhood and becoming a mother myself. She has a fun-to-watch, outrageous personality and a love for her son that is both undeniable and inspirational. In 2003, I was lucky enough to spend a day with her on the set of *Less than Perfect,* and my years-long admiration couldn't help but grow.

I was invited to do a cameo. A nervous wreck, I was way out of my element, but I decided to try to enjoy the opportunity I was being afforded in sharing space on a Hollywood set with comedians who made me laugh every week through my TV. Jenny had a recurring role that season as Dani, the best friend of the main character, Claude, played by the show's star, Sara Rue. In the scene, Claude and Dani find me trying on wedding gowns in a bridal boutique—inspired by my real-life upcoming wedding. I will never forget how at ease I felt with the gracious and hysterical encouragement of Sara and Jenny, who must've been so annoyed with my complete lack of acting ability.

Sometime later, I became friends with Jenny's sister Amy, who married my and Ryan's friend Dan Hinote. Other than their wedding, I haven't had any connection to Jenny except maybe appearing in a tabloid in the same week. She has been a big influence, though. After seeing an interview with her for her autism organization, Generation Rescue, I found a wealth of knowledge on the website and proactively used it as a guide for individualizing the timing of my kids' immunizations.

Much later, I happened to come upon a blog post Jenny wrote called " . . . And I Lived Happily Ever After." Sound familiar? Even though I hadn't crossed paths with Jenny in quite some time, she graciously granted permission for me to reprint her piece here. Read below for a sweet example of being given a reason to smile.

Circa 1980: When I was a little girl, I would walk around with my three Cabbage Patch dolls and practice being the greatest mom in the world. I was confident I would have three children and be married to Prince Charming and live happily ever after.

The images in my head of what my future looked like were so real to me that I had trouble differentiating what decade I was in. If time machines were real, I wonder if I would go back to 1980 to tell Jenny to stop that foolish dream? Would I tell her that she would be divorced, have only one child who would be later diagnosed with something called autism and be left to financially cover all of the bills and caretaking on her own? Probably not. I prefer surprises anyway.

Even though my fairy tale didn't come true the way I imagined it, I was able to shift my thinking from victim to warrior. With age came realization that whatever cards I was dealt it was up to me to decide to live in a happily-ever-after state of mind or a woe-is-me one. Don't get me wrong, I get in my fair share of pity parties, but my time spent in them lessens as I get older. I have also learned to focus on what I have instead of what I don't have. My thoughts went from, "I never did have three kids" to "I'm so lucky to have just Evan." I find the blessing in the fact that I don't have to split my attention. I can spoil him with all the love in my heart. Sure, I would have loved two more, but to argue with reality is to argue with God.

(Reprinted with permission from *Splash* by the *Chicago Sun-Times*)

I, for one, love a good debate, but I agree with Jenny—attempting a debate with God is not my idea of intelligent. Throughout our lives, we may question how and why we end up where we end up, but only when we reach the different stops along our path can we look back and get our answers. We need to trust in the power of the big picture and accept that our expectations won't always be realized as we envision them. As the athlete Maurice Setter once said, "Too many people miss the silver lining because they are expecting gold."

Life is full of delays and pit stops, accidents and detours. All we can do is hold on tight and appreciate the blessings that show up along the way—especially the ones that show up unpredictably and were put in place to give us the greatest joy.

FATEFUL CHANGE

As I've mentioned in numerous sections of this book, my husband is one of the most dedicated and honorable people I know—two of the many reasons why I love him and

wanted him to be the father of my children. Drawn to doing something with his life that would allow him to keep his
favorite community safe as well as stimulate him mentally
and challenge him physically, he became a firefighter in Vail,
Colorado. However, if his aspirations had panned out as he
had hoped, his trajectory would've been very different—and
I don't believe it would've included our happy family. Instead
of being admired by his adoring wife and children and dedicating himself to a community and career he loves, he most
likely would've been admired by adoring fans of football and
dedicating himself to a game he has loved since he was three
years old.

No, we don't have a room in our house dedicated to the
Broncos or a son named Walter Payton in honor of Ryan's favorite player growing up, but nonetheless it's a game Ryan has
fond memories of and one that he consistently excelled at.

After walking on (the term used when you have not
been actively recruited) to the University of Colorado Buffaloes in 1993, he proved his worth to all the college scouts
who hadn't taken a chance on him, winning Special Teams
Player of the Year three times, being named All-Conference
and Defensive MVP, and to this day, still holding the record
for the second most tackles in a season. A strong architec-
ture student, Ryan knew he could follow in his father's professional footsteps, but as a pick in the fifth round of the
1998 NFL draft, he decided to pursue his dream of playing
professional football instead and signed with the Baltimore
Ravens. His time there was short-lived, as he was released at
the end of training camp, but he was quickly picked up by
the Carolina Panthers and after ten weeks on the practice
squad was put on the active roster. Listed as a starter in a

game against the New York Jets, Ryan found himself on the field awaiting the opening kickoff. His first game with the world watching—one he had waited for nearly all his life, and after nine seconds, it was over.

Ryan had dived out trying to trip up the player returning the kickoff and tore all the ligaments of his shoulder and his rotator cuff muscle clear off the bone. Two days later, he was in surgery and for the rest of the season, he was in rehab. Released when the season ended, he got picked up by the Seattle Seahawks but was released after a couple weeks. He ended his career after one season with the Barcelona Dragons in 2000, never having completely recovered from his initial injury.

Had he not been injured on his very first play, I can't imagine that he wouldn't have continued to climb the NFL ladder of success (yes, I'm biased, but it's true—he's annoyingly good at everything he does!). As fate would have it, though, he decided to trade in his football helmet for a fire helmet, and thankfully so. His new path led him straight into my arms and straight into a profession that I know has directly benefited from his hardworking spirit. He has helped more people than I can count and has no plans to stop anytime soon, although he did have the chance back in 2004.

Feeling more fit and healthy than he had in years, thanks to his training for the Ironman triathlon in Kona, Hawaii, Ryan got a second chance to make his NFL dreams come true. After pondering the odds that he could make a comeback in the world of football and redeem his nine-second history, he sent an e-mail to his previous sports agent, Peter Schaffer, to get his thoughts. Without hesitation, Peter reached out to his NFL contacts and heard back from the New Orleans Saints coaching staff. They remembered Ryan from his success with the CU Buffaloes and wanted to fly him out for a tryout with the coaches and scouts. He did so well that they invited him back for minicamp, where he impressed the decision makers so much that they planned to offer him a free-agent contract at the end of the second and final day.

If only the universe had cooperated.

During the first drill of the afternoon, Ryan took off running down the field to cover a punt and was stopped in his tracks. Unable to walk, he quickly realized that history was repeating itself. With only a few hours left of minicamp, the team's medical staff confirmed that he wouldn't be playing anymore that day or anymore, period. He had completely ruptured his Achilles tendon.

There's no way to know whether Ryan's torn Achilles sent him down a better or a worse path in life. What I do know is that, over and over again, the universe nudged him toward redefining his occupational dreams, solidifying the answers to the questions of what he was meant to do and where he was meant to be. He was meant to be with me. He was meant to be a wonderful father to Max and Blakesley. He was meant to live in the Vail Valley and do his part to keep its residents safe. As the Roman Emperor Marcus Aurelius said almost 2,000 years ago, "Accept whatever comes to you woven in the pattern of your destiny, for what could more aptly fit your needs?"

I'm not always happy to have to kiss Ryan good-bye when he leaves for his forty-eight-hour shifts, but I will always be grateful for the change in his trajectory that caused our paths to cross and caused him to seek out a career in which he could literally lend a hand to those in need. I'd say all those he has helped would agree.

SURVIVAL OF THE OPTIMIST

J.R. Martinez (a fellow member of my *Dancing with the Stars* family who ended up doing *much* better than me) dreamed of playing in the NFL from a young age, just like my husband. It's all he remembers wanting to do and all he put his energy into. In fact, he was so fixated on it that he lost focus on the big picture. Lacking certain academic credits, he was told by college faculty during a tour that he wouldn't be eligible to play at the collegiate level for two years. Feeling as though he'd had his life's passion stolen out from under his pigskin-stained fingertips, he stubbornly thought, "If I can't play college sports, then I won't go to college."

That summer, he sat around feeling sorry for himself. He'd just turned nineteen years old, and the worst thing that could have happened to him did. The. Worst. Thing.

Or so he thought.

While wasting away that summer on his couch, feeling that the whole world was against him, he saw a commercial that would change his life. The army was looking for a few good men and women to serve our great country. He remembered the recruiters who had visited his high school earlier that year, and he reached out to a couple of coaches he knew and respected who had been in the military. In speaking with them, he realized that he could give back to a country that had only the year before been terrorized on September 11, travel, earn money for college, and get the credits he needed to play four years of football. He decided that it was the perfect detour and he ended up enlisting.

After basic training, J.R. reported to Fort Campbell, Kentucky. It was January 2003 and with American troops gearing up to invade Iraq, he knew going to war was a possibility—he just didn't think he would be part of it. But a few weeks later, he received his orders—his unit would be deployed to the war zone—and by March he found himself looking out at the desert of Kuwait City.

Early on, his unit's assignment was relatively simple: patrolling the southern region of Iraq and escorting military personnel such as cooks and medics from point A to point B. On April 5, 2003, they received another routine assignment, but at the last minute their mission suddenly changed. J.R. found himself driving a Humvee in a convoy headed along a route that hadn't been cleared. When the route changed, his world changed.

Unknowingly, J.R. had driven over a roadside bomb—not only detonating it, but also detonating everything they had inside the vehicle, including extra fuel and ammunition. The force of the explosion ejected the other three soldiers from the truck and engulfed it in flames—with J.R. helplessly trapped inside, literally burning alive.

Completely conscious, he suffered unspeakable pain for five of the longest minutes of his life. He could've easily succumbed to the temptation he was feeling to close his eyes and give in to his weakening body, but instead, he thought of his mother and made a choice to fight.

You just hold on. You keep yourself alive! he told himself. He screamed and yelled at the top of his lungs to keep himself awake until he was finally pulled from the flames by two of his courageous sergeants.

When the helicopter arrived to carry him to safety, he was immediately put into a medically induced coma and flown to a military hospital in Germany so he could receive treatment to ward off infection and repair his damaged lungs and internal organs from extreme inhalation injuries. He had also been burned over 34 percent of his body and required immediate surgery—the first of thirty-four he has had to date. *Thirty-four surgeries.*

When he was stable, he was transferred to the Brooke Army Medical Center in San Antonio, Texas, where he was taken out of his induced coma. He had been asleep for three and a half weeks and was understandably confused, but through the sea of people with protective masks and gear on, he immediately recognized the tear-filled eyes of his mother, his sole inspiration to stay alive. Speaking his first words in almost a month, J.R. reminded his mother of what he had said when he left for Iraq: "One way or another, I'm going to come home." And come home, he did. If only home had actually been his house and not the hospital room where he would stay for three months, or nearby living quarters that he would call home for three long years during his difficult recovery.

He received excellent care, but it was intensely painful care, with daily treatments and frequent surgeries that were more incapacitating and excruciating than the explosion itself. He celebrated his twentieth, twenty-first, and twenty-second birthdays at Brooke Army Medical Center, where he learned all about the depths of depression and the stages of grief—especially the stage of anger.

J.R. was angry that he would never be able to return to football or the military career that he had subsequently fallen in love with. When he saw his face for the first time, he was angry that he would have to live the rest of his life so visibly scarred in a world so based on looks. He was angry at the thought of never finding a wife or having children. He was angry that, even with his mother's love and support, he felt completely alone.

After all, no one would ever go through the same thing and understand him . . . ever. No one. No way.

But as J.R. learned about six months after he was trapped in that fiery Humvee, he was anything but alone. With his mother's help, he was finally able to see the light of positivity.

"I don't know *why you* and I don't know *why us*," she told him, "but we have to be strong. In time it will start to make sense."

When it finally registered that, like his mother, who had suffered greatly in her life, he had a choice, J.R. was presented with an opportunity. One of his nurses asked him to visit another patient who had also been injured in Iraq. She was hoping that J.R. could talk to him about the recovery process and let him know that he wasn't alone. This fellow soldier was having a very difficult time. Although J.R. could easily empathize with his condition, he was apprehensive about entering his room, especially knowing how fragile he himself had felt at that early stage. The last thing J.R. wanted to do was to go in there and push this man further into his own darkness. But with a little encouragement from the nurse, he decided to give it a go and honor her request.

As soon as he entered the room, J.R. noticed the darkness. The room was silent, the lights were off, and the blinds were closed. J.R. sensed this wasn't just to protect the room from the sweltering heat of the Texas summer. After introducing himself, J.R. told the soldier why he was there, and they started a conversation about life, a conversation that lasted forty minutes longer than he expected. As J.R. left the room, he suggested that they talk again the next day.

"I'd appreciate that," his new friend said.

What happened next was so simple and yet so profound—the wounded soldier turned on the lights and opened the curtains.

At that moment, J.R. physically felt the impact of sharing his story. He knew that he had helped this new patient, whether it was to brighten his mood or brighten his perspective, and he wanted to do it again, and again, and again for whomever else he could help.

Every day, after J.R. completed his own treatments, he went on his rounds, visiting other patients. The opportunity to serve his country as a soldier had been taken away, but by sharing his experience with fellow patients, he realized that he still had the opportunity to serve and to inspire, and on a much more personal level.

Thankfully for everyone who has come to know him or about him, J.R.'s ability to inspire has grown far past the walls of the hospital. He became a motivational speaker; an actor on the daytime drama *All My Children*, in which he was cast in the role of an actual veteran; the winner of the thirteenth season of *Dancing with the Stars*; the author of a best-selling memoir, *Full of Heart: My Story of Survival, Strength, and Spirit*; and now the host of his own Newstalk radio show. To date, J.R. has shared his story with millions of people, and I have no doubt he'll touch millions more lives in the years to come.

Through his tragic experience, J.R. found meaning, just as his mom once assured him he would. With a purpose bigger than himself, he connects to others daily, letting them know that they have a choice in life. He tells people that you can choose to see your circumstances as a curse or a blessing, regardless of whether you usually lean toward optimism or pessimism. And after living through the stuff that nightmares are made of, J.R. Martinez has had every reason to succumb to the anger and pain and darkness and exist as a pessimist for the rest of his life. Instead, he has chosen to see the explosion as a blessing. He has chosen to survive and thrive, to be grateful and inspire. With the help of his mother and the flick of a light switch, J.R. made a choice to fight for himself and for other victims instead of fighting against his circumstances and the world.

And if he can, we all can.

A BODY OF BLESSINGS

Many people dedicate their lives to careers that save lives. They are first responders and life-flight pilots; nurses, doctors, and surgeons; chemists and philanthropists; police officers and soldiers . . . and the list goes on. We rely on them to heal us, answer the calls we make to 911, protect us from violence, and fight our wars. They are the true heroes.

Sometimes, though, heroes come from more "ordinary" walks of life. After hearing the story of Jamie Bradfield, the owner of a construction company, I couldn't help but think of him as one of those extraordinary "ordinary" heroes—a hero who found the path to a lifelong blessing.

It was in the fall of 2012 that Jamie first connected with Thomas Jones. Thomas's family had been members of the same church Jamie's family attended for two years, but up until then Jamie had met them only in passing. One Sunday morning before delivering his sermon, the pastor at First United Methodist Church in LaGrange, Georgia, informed the congregation that ten-year-old Thomas needed a new kidney. The family was looking for people with Type O blood to get tested as a possible match to save this boy, born with a genetic kidney disease. With a new organ, he could say good-bye to ten-hour daily dialysis treatments and actually have a childhood—and a future.

Initially, Jamie (who has O-positive blood) didn't respond, but over the course of the next month, he kept reading the notices in the church bulletins and newsletters calling for willing applicants. He thought: What the heck? What are the odds?

So Jamie had his blood drawn, and a couple weeks later he learned he was a match. With another applicant ahead of him in line, he figured he had missed the boat, so he went back to his life. A month went by. Then Jamie got a call from a nurse at the hospital, explaining that after the second round of testing, the first applicant wasn't an option anymore. She asked if he would still be willing to proceed. In that moment, his decision became real and time stood still.

Jamie's mind flashed back to eleven years earlier when he and his wife, Claire, were doing anything and everything they could to become parents for the second time.

After being told for most of her adult life that Claire would be physically incapable of having children, they had hearts full of hope that God would bless them with another miracle, just as He had their daughter, Sara Kate, who was conceived the old-fashioned way only ten months into their marriage. Jamie and Claire then continued to try for seven long years to get the news that they were once again pregnant. "We did in-vitro fertilization and a host of other methods to get pregnant, and all we got was financially strapped," he said. Finally, they accepted that they were a one-child family, and moved on. As is often the case, once they had given up, Claire found out she was pregnant. However, when they went in for the first ultrasound at ten weeks, the obstetrician could find only "clutter." He speculated that she had miscarried and recommended scheduling a D & C, a procedure that would clean out her uterus. But when pressed, the doctor conceded he wasn't 100 percent certain that the baby wasn't still alive. Without certainty, Jamie and Claire were having a difficult time believing that it was God's plan that they lose this precious gift. Recognizing their pain, the doctor suggested that they wait another week and then come in for another ultrasound. They agreed.

After five days, though, Jamie's anxious wife couldn't stand the suspense any longer and they called their doctor. Making time for them to come in that day, Claire's obstetrician arranged to do the ultrasound and proactively scheduled a visit to the operating room for the D & C right after that—just in case.

When Jamie and Claire got to the office, the atmosphere was funereal, with nurses crying and the doctor somber. But the mood instantly changed from sadness to joy when the ultrasound immediately showed a strong heartbeat!

Now, flash forward to the moment that time stood still. Jamie didn't know the little boy who needed a kidney that well, but he did know he was the same age as Sam, the child Jamie and Claire believe God miraculously gave back to them ten years earlier. That's all it took. On January 3, 2013, Jamie gave one of his kidneys to that little boy.

In a Christmas letter Jamie sent out to his friends and family shortly before the surgery, he wrote:

"Know that all you have is a gift from God and give thanks for those gifts. If you have the opportunity to do good for someone else, do it! It may not be the gift of an organ, but I am sure there will be other opportunities. The gifts you will receive in return will be immeasurable."

For ten years, Jamie and Thomas were virtual strangers. They traveled in similar community circles, but with a thirty-eight-year age difference, they had no natural reason to connect. A horrible disease, a caring church, a healthy "spare" kidney, a matching blood type, and a heart full of generosity bound them so much that they now consider each other friends.

Lifelong friends.

And even after Jamie endured painful medical procedures that left permanent scars, the positives for him far surpassed the negatives: he was able to give the gift of quality of life to a boy who was finally able to experience a world beyond the hospital walls. It was a path Jamie hadn't considered until that fateful day at church, but one he is forevermore grateful to have been a part of.

PROFESSIONAL SACRIFICE AND PERSONAL REWARD

In the blended and mostly harmonious family known as *The Bachelor* franchise, we bond over shared experiences and the bizarre world we live in where millions of strangers tune in weekly to watch our unconventional love stories unfold. Not only did I find my true love and my destiny through the show, but I've been lucky enough to add household names like Chris Harrison, Jillian Harris, Andrew Firestone,

Emily Maynard, Ashley Hebert, and Sean Lowe to my list of friends. Some of my strongest connections, though, are with people from behind the scenes. They are the producers, director, set designers, stylists, camera operators, and even sound technicians whose job is to create a show that people will want to watch. Sometimes their agendas don't align with the "talent," but I respect that they have a job to do, and at the very least, many of them are good (*very* good, in fact) at comedic relief.

Karri-Leigh Mastrangelo is one of those people. She didn't come on board Mike Fleiss's production team until I was an old married broad, but we met when she was expecting a baby and helping prepare us to show off our own baby on an *After the Final Rose* special—and we instantly clicked. Through the years, we've stayed in touch—mostly when it involved appearances I made with the franchise, but now that she has moved on to produce other shows, we bond over how entertaining it is to be a parent and encourage each other with the different projects we find on our plates.

Contemplating a foray into the world of blogging, Karri-Leigh (KL to me) reached out to me for advice. I had only a tiny amount of experience with this relatively new medium, but productive-mom-to-productive-mom, I was happy to offer my insights. Without knowing what she would title it or what she would write about, I knew without a doubt that she would offer the blogosphere a fresh and witty perspective on life, Hollywood, and parenthood, and I was right. For two years now, she has written tons of posts and has attracted a huge number of readers.

One of those blog posts caught my eye. I was hard at work on this book and I had a big problem: writer's block. Taking a break from writing, I sat down to go through my e-mail, and Karri-Leigh's latest post on her Dirty Laundry & Dirty Diapers website popped up. Not only did this break give me some energy, but it also offered a perfect illustration of the gratitude we feel from the surprises hidden in our professional journey. Thankfully, KL happily agreed to let me reprint the post here, while graciously adding a few more tidbits just for your reading pleasure. (Thanks, KL, and thank you to Diane Sawyer for pointing her in my direction.)

I'm often asked how I got into television. The truth is that I grew up wanting to be a child psychologist. In college, I started out studying elementary education for moderate special needs, but I knew after my very first rotation as a student teacher in the second grade of an affluent Massachusetts town that the field wasn't for me. The job saddened me. One beautiful girl, barely seven years old, suffered from liver issues. Her classmate, consistently late to school, wasn't distracted by cartoons but by his alcoholic mother—and this wasn't even the special needs room.

The teacher whom I was supporting told me that in her first years of teaching she dreaded Friday afternoons, as she'd miss and worry about her students over the weekend. Unlike the vast majority of professionals, she could hardly wait for Monday morning to arrive. "If you don't feel that way, this isn't the job for you," she said. Clearly, it wasn't the job for me.

Next on my list of who I wanted to be when I grew up was Diane Sawyer. So I changed my major, made a great demo reel, and wasted an obnoxious amount of money on headshots.

My very first job was at a production company housed in Boston's ABC affiliate, WCVB. I knew from the moment I stepped into their newsroom that the energy behind the camera, not in front of it, was what I craved. Immediately I pursued producing, with great success, but part of me often wondered if I had made the right decision.

A few years, a cross-country move and a marriage later, my passion brought me to Los Angeles. Making my mark in television wasn't easy, but eventually the hard work paid off. I was offered the chance to work on a groundbreaking show called *Welcome to the Neighborhood* for ABC. I was more than willing and ready to take on the challenge, but, still a newlywed, committing to living for the next several months in Austin, Texas, was not an easy decision. Ultimately, I asked for (and received) my husband's support and set out to verify whether this was truly the best professional path for me. I made the supreme sacrifice. I left my entire life behind and crossed my fingers that I wouldn't lose it all in the process.

After months of casting and preparation, principal shooting began. Several "diverse" but upstanding families would compete to win a home in a very white, Christian, and Republican neighborhood—a home they otherwise would never be able to afford, in a place where they may not have been welcome. Time flew by and in no time at all we were shooting our first elimination with a family of professional tattoo artists.

Shuffled off into their exit interviews, they were feeling unwanted and dejected. I held the hand of their beautiful six-year-old daughter—ready to get her perspective on film.

She sat on the curb while I sat on the pavement, and I asked her why she thought her family was the first to be sent home. She had yet to enter the first grade, but spoke more eloquently than most high school graduates. We cried together as she expressed how hard it is to have people make assumptions about her parents based solely upon their looks. I knew in that moment that I was doing what I was meant to do. I was having my producer cake and therapeutically eating it too.

Unfortunately, the world didn't get to see that interview—or any of the incredible stories that proceeded to unfold, for that matter. Hours before our premiere, the National Fair Housing Alliance threatened to sue ABC on the grounds that the show violated anti-discrimination housing laws. Sadly, it was shelved.

My heart truly broke. Professionally, I cried because an incredible social experiment, in which everyday people opened up their homes, hearts, and minds in an effort to break down prejudices way too common in this country, would have a fraction of the outreach it deserved. Selfishly, I cried because the many personal struggles I had endured for the project had seemingly been for naught. Or had they?

The gay couple who won the Austin home in the end still got to share it with their adopted son. They have since married, and adopted once more. I still hear from the previously narrow-minded families who lived in the neighborhood, who reflect upon the experience as mind-opening and transformative. As for the innocent six-year-old, we've long lost touch, but I think of her often. Years after that interview, its camera operator referred me for a job that would again be a life-changing experience—it took me to *The Bachelor,* which, ultimately, brought me to cherished friendships and memories, and a blog for you.

Difficult as it may be, often we must wait until an event has long passed before we can fully understand or even appreciate its purpose. Thankfully, it can be well worth the wait.

True that, Karri-Leigh. True that.

HAPPILY EVER ACTIONS

- If you aren't able to find any meaning or blessing or shiny silver lining in the wounds of a tragedy, and it's hard to contemplate moving forward, start by thinking of the people who love you and need you. Then, little by little turn to the simple things. Get out of bed, brush your teeth, get dressed. Attempt to make progress each day, opening your door, then stepping outside, maybe taking a short walk or getting in your car for a drive. Over time, those steps you take toward actively participating in life will hopefully give you back your life—a life that may not have all the answers, but one filled with blessings big and small.

- We all may not have the willpower or the courage to donate an organ while still living, let alone at the time of our death, but if you can handle a little pinprick and some pressure for a few minutes,

donating blood or bone marrow can be just as powerful. Just ask James Harrison, aka the "man with
the golden arm." An Australian who needed thirteen liters of blood during a major chest surgery he
survived when he was thirteen years old, Harrison
vowed to start donating blood when he turned eighteen as a way to give back. Shortly after his initial
donation, they determined that his blood contained
the Rhesus disease antibody, and it has since been
used to save more than 2.4 million babies, including
his own daughter. I'd say that's pretty damn powerful. To find out more about how you can help someone through donating blood, visit RedCrossBlood
.org, or if you are interested in swabbing your cheek
to find out if you could be a bone marrow match,
visit my friends at LoveHopeStrength.org and click
"Get On the List." You are more powerful than you
think.

≈ Do you constantly fret about disasters—either natural or man-made? Think back over your life to the
moment that fear began. Was it a near-miss or was
it a direct impact? Either way, remember that fear
is what you make of it. No matter how disastrous
events in your past have been, you have the power
to choose your reaction to those events in the present and pave the way toward a fearless future.

≈ Sit back and think about the three most difficult
events of your life. Now think about the domino effects that they caused, focusing on even the faintest

glimmers of light that were generated as a result, and write them down. Maybe the loss of a loved one caused you to empathize with someone struggling with the same issue; maybe you made a donation to a charitable organization that helped others in a similar boat; or maybe an injury led you down a new road that you would've missed if not for your painful circumstance. Don't let the cloud of despair overwhelm you; instead look (very closely) for the sun and the stars undeniably shining behind it. Light exists in the darkness—we just need to adjust our eyes to see it.

"Thank You" Is a Verb

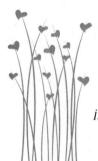

Feeling gratitude and not expressing it
is like wrapping a present and not giving it.

—WILLIAM ARTHUR WARD

I F YOU'VE REACHED THIS PART IN THE BOOK, I HOPE YOU have it ingrained in your mind that gratitude and happiness go hand-in-hand. It improves your outlook and well-being and, as the *Huffington Post* recently reported, it can also help you sleep better, strengthen your relationships, increase life satisfaction, boost immunity, and decrease stress.

But feeling grateful is not quite enough—you've got to put it out there into the universe and let the people you appreciate hear it. There's no doubt the recipient of your thanks will feel great, but many studies show that when you share your gratitude you also share in the joy. So, if you are ready to start sharing, check out some of my favorite ways to say thank you below.

Write a Note

There's something about a handwritten note that makes people feel special. Even though it takes more time than a quick text, a phone call, or an e-mail covered in smiley faces (and if you have been a recipient of my e-mails, you know I am a repeat offender), a personally penned message sent through the good ol' post office is worth the extra effort.

When someone does a kindness for me or for my family, I never worry that a written note of thanks is wrong. It may need to be accompanied by a thoughtful gift or reciprocated action, but the heartwarming feeling of opening a letter sent in the mail isn't something that gets lost on many people.

· With my crazy schedule, it may take quite a bit of time for thank-you notes to reach the top of my priority list, so I've devised a system to ensure they get done. Any time someone does something caring or sends something special for the kids, Ryan, or me, I immediately place a blank note card and the person's address into my thank-you folder. Yes, I have a thank-you folder. Since my memory is less than stellar, my thank-you-note folder ensures that I won't forget any important kindnesses that our family has been blessed to receive (at least in theory). It may be months before I write the note, but I know I'll get there eventually, and, hopefully, when I do, the recipient will realize the sincerity of my thanks.

According to Emily Post, "Handwritten notes are warmer and more personal than a phone call or email, and only second best to thanking someone in person." EmilyPost.com says that if you've gotten a gift for your wedding or shower, birthday, graduation, promotion, or any other reason, send a note. Likewise, a note or gift because someone thought of you when you were ill or in mourning warrants a handwritten note of thanks.

If people take time out of their busy lives to let you know they care, you can do the same, can't you?

Of course, as someone who easily forgets what day it is unless I'm looking at a calendar, I know it can be difficult to remember and even harder to find the time to sit down undisturbed and write a thoughtful expression of gratitude. That's why I bring my handy-dandy folder with me on planes (at least those that happen to be free of two mini Sutters), on road trips, to doctor appointments and visits to the hair salon, and any time I know I am going to be, or can be, sitting in one place for at least a few minutes without having to feed a hungry mouth or escort a tiny human to the bathroom. It's all about time management and taking advantage of what precious time I have to cross things off the list.

Here's the rundown: First, I make sure to choose appropriate stationery. If I'm responding to a kindness shown to our family of four, I reach for the personalized "The Sutters" note cards. If I'm writing someone who has done something nice for me, Ryan, Max, or Blakesley individually, I use customized cards for each of us. That's not to say that cards you buy in bulk at Costco or Walmart or your local gift shop won't do the trick (I have lots of those for when I run out of the personalized goodies), but I have a bit of an infatuation with pretty paper and think it gives the card that little extra touch. I then address and stamp the corresponding envelope and stuff it in my collection folder with a pen and the notepad where I keep track of all the notes I've written in the past few years. That way, when I find the time to write, it's all right there in one spot. Keeping track may seem incredibly silly, but I've been known to write someone twice, and although it may be doubly nice, it's also a waste of time (and embarrassing to boot).

For some fun examples of how to go about writing a thoughtful note of thanks, as well as my favorite paper sources, flip through to the "Resource-full" chapter at the end of the book . . . but make sure to come back and finish the rest!

Send an E-mail

Although I don't think traditional etiquette experts would approve, times have changed, and at certain moments, an e-mail will do the trick for expressing your thanks. I'm a huge fan of websites like Smilebox.com and PaperlessPost. com, but even without their help of designer virtual greetings, a sincerely written message sent via e-mail is a great runner-up option.

Take the story of my friend Ellen. A few years ago, her ex-husband's mother passed away. Ellen hadn't seen her former in-laws since she separated from her husband about five years earlier, but her mother-in-law in particular remained very near and dear to her heart. Throughout the ten years Ellen was part of that family, her mother-in-law had embraced her like a long-lost daughter. Knowing how Ellen felt about his mom, her ex was kind enough to call her the morning the older woman died. His sister, Ellen's former sister-in-law, subsequently let her know when and where the wake and funeral would take place. So, as potentially awkward as it would be for Ellen to show up, especially because her ex-husband had a new life with a new wife and baby by then, she gathered up the courage to pay her respects.

When Ellen arrived at the wake, she was surprised by the (mostly) welcoming and lovely attitude of her former family members—even receiving an invitation to dinner with them afterward. The next day at the church, though, was noticeably different. During the funeral service, the family gathered in the front pews, as is custom, and Ellen found herself sitting alone near the back of the church. She told me that it was about the loneliest she has ever felt.

At the end of the service, the people Ellen used to call family walked out behind the casket, with friends and acquaintances following behind. One woman she had known back in high school looked over at her, saw what a wreck she was, and stepped out of the procession to give her a hug and say, "I know how much she meant to you." Ellen described it as one of the most amazing things anyone had ever done for her—a simple gesture, yet incredibly poignant and appreciated.

When Ellen got home, the first thing she did was try to track down this old acquaintance's e-mail address. When she found it, she sent along her sincere thanks. No matter what she did to thank this woman for her gesture, Ellen knows that it couldn't match the effect it had on her. Though it was one of the saddest days she has ever experienced, a woman she knew back in high school saved it from being one of total devastation. Ellen knows her method of thanks wasn't Emily Post–worthy, but in a world of instant messages at your fingertips, Ellen did the best she could. Sometimes that's all you can do.

Reach Out and Touch Someone

My mom will gladly tell you that her favorite thing is a hug. In fact, you could call my entire family "huggers." For us, it's an instant way of connecting with the ones we love and showing that we care. But hugs don't have to be limited to family or close friends. They can also be a heartfelt way of expressing gratitude to a nurse who cared for you in the hospital or a hairstylist who gave you the potential for a month of good hair days. We all know how to use our arms, so don't be shy—just do it!

And if body contact is a little too close for comfort, why not try the age-old tradition of a handshake. I remember sitting in the theater as the movie *Argo* was coming to a close. I won't give away the surprises, but the film is based on a true story about what one man and our government did to save the lives of a group of diplomats trapped in Iran. (I *highly* recommend it!) I realize that what I was seeing and hearing on the movie screen was being performed by actors who had been given a set dialogue of lines, but one particular scene seemed so authentic and so perfectly fitted to this type of thanks that I had to share.

One of the diplomats, who hadn't been especially kind to the man who was trying to save him, realized that he owed his rescuer a genuine gesture of gratitude. So he approached him and simply reached out his hand.

No words were spoken, only handshakes exchanged.

In shaking his hand, he modestly communicated his thanks in a touching way—something any one of us could do in real life.

Share a Favorite Treat

Every circumstance calls for a specific action, and sometimes a handshake, hug, or thank you via snail mail or electronic mail just doesn't cut it. When someone goes above and beyond the call of duty as a friend or coworker or family member, they deserve a note that accompanies something bigger, better, and maybe even tastier. When Molly Mesnick (the beautiful wife of Jason Mesnick) helped me bring to life a philanthropic idea, her hard work deserved much more than a note.

Time to rewind . . .

I reached out to her and a group of folks I knew from my television family of *The Bachelor* and *The Bachelorette* for their thoughts on gathering together clothing and accessories we had all worn while appearing on the ABC shows and auctioning off the items for a good cause. I had always felt that my televised outfits were meant for much more than collecting dust in my closet, even if they weren't quite up to par with the current stylish standards of the show, and they could raise much-needed money for any number of different charities. Molly immediately agreed and offered her support. She connected me with the like-minded folks at eDrop-Off, who helped us create an event in Chicago that raised $10,000 for the American Red Cross. I was ecstatic! Without Molly's help (or everybody at eDrop-Off or all the Bachelors and Bachelorettes who donated their goodies), though, I couldn't have turned my vision into reality.

I didn't feel like a note or e-mail would do the trick alone, and since we had just celebrated the success of the event in the Windy City, I knew she would appreciate an old Chicago staple of deliciousness—Garrett popcorn—so I sent her a tin of my favorite combo. In this case, it's not necessarily just the thought that counts. Think about flavor, presentation, and whether it will stay fresh on a trip across the country, and try not to get jealous of what they will soon be devouring. If you are, though, you can always order yourself a little treat at the same time!

Bloom Where You Are Planted

Nothing is quite like getting a knock on the door and opening it to find someone from your favorite flower shop obscured by a beautiful arrangement of flowers. I recently received a small but stunning floral gift from my friends at the Vail Valley Medical Center after doing my best to raise funds for their second annual "Pink Vail" fund-raiser. I had received verbal and electronic thank-yous from their staff for the donations I was able to elicit, which would help fund programs at the Shaw Regional Cancer Center, but I was pleasantly surprised that they would take the time to seek out my favorite flower shop (VailVintageMagnolia.com) and have them put together something just for me. Every time I walked by our dining room table, sat down to eat, or caught a glimpse of the roses, cabbage, greenery, and purple cremon from another room, I smiled. The flowers may not have lasted forever, but I will always remember their beauty and the thoughtfulness that brought them my way.

Use Your Words

In the movie *I Don't Know How She Does It,* Sarah Jessica Parker's character is teased for constantly saying thank you. Of course, it was a movie peopled with made-up characters, but it was surprising to me that anyone would ever think that you could say those two important words too much, unless it was consistently insincere. And since notes or gifts aren't necessary, say the experts, when it comes to thanking your husband for picking up the mail or your father-in-law for taking out the trash, I make sure to show my thanks verbally as often as possible. I believe that more is more when it comes to expressing your gratitude (clearly, or I wouldn't have written this book), so I say it as many times as I can and I encourage you to do the same. The words "thank you" never get old.

They may even be a welcome change, especially for those working in the service industry. Think about how many times you contact the manager or customer service department of a company with a complaint, compared with the number of calls you make to praise someone for a job well done.

My friend Renee once called a pizza place to speak with the management after the staff went to great lengths to correct a messed-up order. The manager answered the phone in a tone that made her envision him thinking, "What am I going to be yelled at about this time?" Instead, Renee told him that she just wanted to thank them for going the extra mile. After a long pause, the manager said, "No one ever says thank you. That's really great that you called." Did it change the world? No. But it reminded her to express appreciation for even the small things. If I were a betting woman, I would wager that it probably stuck with that guy too. As Margaret Cousins, a writer and editor, once said, "Appreciation can make a day, even change a life. Your willingness to put it into words is all that is necessary."

So, if someone offers you exceptional service or even service accompanied by a rare smile, speak up and let them know you were paying attention.

Tip Away

My friend Liz lives in New Jersey—one of only two states in the US that does not allow you to pump your own gas at gas stations. For most of her life, though, she lived in New York, where full service was a choice. If you chose to request assistance in filling up your tank, it was customary to offer that person a tip.

When she moved to New Jersey, the tipping habits she established in New York had been solidified, and Liz continued to give the attendant a dollar whenever she got gas. She was shocked by the huge smiles they would give her in return—it was a buck, for cryin' out loud. Yes, it was their job to fuel up the cars that came through the station, but, like sticking something in the tip jars at your local coffee or sandwich shop or leaving a little cash behind for the housekeeping staff of your hotel, a monetary recognition of thanks isn't necessary. It's just nice.

Tweet, Tweet

For whatever reasons, more people take the time to complain than the time to praise, especially in our generation of social media. The Touch Agency reported that of the over 1 billion new Twitter posts each week during 2011, about 80 percent of those that related to customer service were critical. That's a lot of negativity.

Crying foul is certainly important in making sure to hold people and companies accountable, but even more important is providing praise for praiseworthy actions. Think of the Golden Rule: treat others how you'd like to be treated and don't hold back when you receive excellent service.

You may tell a manager how much you appreciate her hard work over the phone or in person, fill out a questionnaire and send it via snail mail, or e-mail a customer service rep, but in today's age of technological connections to companies around the world, social media offers something the other options can't: the ability to shout it from computerized rooftops.

With the help of sites like Twitter, Facebook, and Google Plus, you can write up a review of your experience, click send, and in less than a nanosecond (or maybe a tad longer depending on whether the connection gods are happy with you), you can share your opinion with anyone who will listen, including the company you are pleasantly shouting about.

By connecting the social-media dots between your friends, family, and followers with worthy companies deserving of their attention, you are saying thank you in the most far-reaching and potentially valuable way. Take advantage and make someone's day (and maybe make your own in the process).

SHARED WEALTH

Knowing that I am by far not the end-all and be-all on the topic of expressing appreciation, I reached out to my virtual family and friends and asked their favorite ways to spread the love. Here are some of the standouts:

- Jennifer Kimball: "We have a cute glass jar we keep in the kitchen. We place notes in the jar that capture little moments we have throughout the year that we are grateful for (fun day, cherished memory, etc.). On New Year's Eve, we open the champagne and read through the notes from the year and look back with gratitude."

Similar to jotting down my favorite part of the day, then recording them in a book that contains my kiddos' sayings and special moments, I am a huge fan of reflecting back on the year with this idea. Thanks, Jennifer!

- Barb Sutter: "Today we just received a gift from a person we stayed with during a vacation we took to Palm Springs. We loved a smoker they had, and lo and behold we got one in the mail. Now . . . were they thanking us for making the trip, or are they just very thoughtful friends?"

I don't know, but regardless, I *love* the idea of thanking someone for taking the time out of their schedule to come visit you with a favorite gift from the trip!

- Patty Borges: "Nothing says thank you like a good baked treat."

So true, Patty. So true.

- Brenda Perry: "My daddy loved to drive, and he drove down a certain road every day, several times a day, until his death at age eighty-seven. My husband and I decided that the best way we could show everyone how much he was appreciated by his family was to adopt the highway where he traveled. So we adopted two stretches along that road and the sign reads 'In Loving Memory of James Graham Roberts.'"

I'm sure he smiles down on you and that sign every day, Brenda.

- Jennifer MacNaughton Carabetta: "One of my favorites is for really good friends, when you know they are coming back from a trip, to have a dinner ready for them and some basics in their fridge. You have to have their house key to do this, but it's the nicest thing ever to get home from traveling with kids and not have to worry about that! It's really just a 'thank you for being my wonderful friend!' kind of thank-you, but you can always make a specific reason."

Great idea, Jennifer!

- Samantha Higgins: "Handwritten thank-you notes and donations to charity in their honor are my top two faves."

Definitely two of my favorites as well . . . especially the charitable donation that keeps the positivity going!

HAPPILY EVER ACTIONS

❧ Order yourself a freshly minted batch of monogrammed stationery either through one of the websites I suggest in the "Resource-full" section or one you have used or had recommended to you. It's a wonder what the gift of paper does and how much you'll want to show it off.

❧ Think of three people who have done you a kindness in the past month, pull out one of your lovely new notes, and try out your sharpened skills. And if you aren't a stranger to the handwritten process, think outside the box about how you can express your appreciation, just as my virtual friends and family did.

❧ Today, make it a point to say thank you to two people. Not just the standard "thanks" you give when someone holds a door open for you or hands you your change, but go above and beyond the norm by sending someone flowers, just because, or posting a positive comment on Facebook about an employee of a local company you use and love.

≈ As John F. Kennedy once said, "As we express our gratitude, we must never forget that the highest appreciation is not to utter words, but to live by them." That said, don't ignore the guidelines of etiquette and forget to formally thank those who show you kindnesses, but remember that the only way to keep a grateful attitude alive is to embody it through your actions.

The Final Rose:
My Thank-You Note
to You

*You can't leave a footprint that lasts
if you're always walking on tiptoe.*

—Marion C. Blakey

OVER THE PAST TEN YEARS, I'VE PUT MYSELF OUT THERE for the world to watch and criticize and judge. At first it was about creating some excitement in my own life and experiencing a new adventure. As my "fifteen minutes" extended, though, my intentions turned instead to love and family and creating a happy future with the man of my dreams.

Along the way, I've had many extraordinary opportunities. I've taken a ride in the Goodyear Blimp; had Ken Paves style my hair for an *O* magazine photo shoot; pet a baby tiger being held by <u>the</u> Jack Hanna; played baseball with my baseball idol, Hall of Fame shortstop Ozzie Smith; been named #7 on *Maxim*'s Hot 100 list; received a few hugs from Oprah; caught a pass from legendary quarterback Doug Flutie; been photographed for a "Got Milk?" ad by David LaChapelle; and had country music star Brad Paisley serenade me and my groom as we danced our first dance to a song my new husband had written me in the form of a poem during our courtship.

Writing this book is now right up there too—even if you are the only person to read it.

When I started posting my "favorite part of the day" on Twitter, my life changed. I had people cheering me on and saying things like: "a day without your favorite part of the day is like a day without sunshine"; and "your fave part of day is something I now look forward to. Love your happy energy. Share the smiles." I realized, through the support of friends and family and followers, that even though I hadn't earned a degree in positive psychology, I still had something to say—something I believed in, could be proud of, and could speak about from an authentic and inspirational place.

That something is gratitude.

In an attempt to make this world shine a little brighter, join me in ending each day by acknowledging your "favorite part of the day." Tweet it. Post it on your Facebook wall. Record it on your phone or write it down. It can be in a fancy antique leather-bound journal, something as simple as a marble composition book, or even a pad of sticky notes. At the end of each day, reflect on what you were grateful to have experienced. If it was one of the best days of your life, you may have a hard time making a choice. If it was one of your most challenging days, you may find that you are thankful merely for being alive. No matter the highs or the lows, there is always something to be thankful for . . . always.

Gratitude is the glue that keeps our feet firmly planted on the ground.

Gratitude is the light that shines when our world is darkened by clouds.

Gratitude keeps us happy and healthy and focused on the little things that make a big difference in our world. Whether it's a clean kitchen, your kids "swimming" in the bathtub, a simple chat with a cousin you've lost touch with, a stopped driver allowing you to cross the street in safety, or a flower growing amid a bed of weeds, we are all surrounded by op-portunities to see the world through the brilliant light of positivity.

I choose optimism.

I choose silver linings.

I choose gratitude.

Resource-full

Happiness is only real when shared.

—CHRIS MCCANDLESS

IN THE PAST TWO HUNDRED-PLUS PAGES, THE STORIES AND scientific research I have shared have all been done so in an effort to introduce you to or enhance the power of your own grateful heart. I am confident that if you embrace gratitude, you will find yourself being embraced by a heightened and more consistent joy. Instead of just asking you to believe me, though, I wanted to include the sources where I found much of my inspiration. Check them out if you don't want the inspiration to stop!

CHAPTER 1

- How being grateful gives us increased energy, optimism, social connections, and happiness:

  — "Thank You. No Thank You: Grateful People Are Happier, Healthier Long After the Leftovers Are Gobbled Up," *Wall Street Journal*, November 23, 2010.

— "Practicing Gratitude Can Increase Happiness by 25%," PsyBlog, September 10, 2007; www.spring.org.uk2007/09 /practicing-gratitude-can-increase.php.

• Amy Biehl's story. Amy Biehl Foundation: AmyBiehl.org. See also excerpts of Paula Zahn's interview with Amy's mom, Linda Biehl, on CNN, December 9, 2004; www.cnn.com/2004/WORLD/africa /12/09/biehl.

Chapter 2

• The benefits of dancing: Lane Anderson, "Mind Your Body: Dance Yourself Happy," *Psychology Today,* July 1, 2010, and Madeline Knight, "9 Benefits of Dance," EverydayHealth.com; www.everydayhealth .com/fitness-pictures/health-benefits-of-dance.aspx#/slide-1.

• The benefits of meditation:

— Adam Hoffman, "Study Reveals Benefits of Meditation," *Brown Daily Herald,* February 22, 2013, citing a study led by Catherine Kerr, assistant professor of family medicine at Alpert Medical School and director of translational neu- roscience for Brown University's Contemplative Studies Initiative; www.browndailyherald.com/2013/02/22/study -reveals-benefits-of-meditation.

— Four additional studies are cited in this blog about a TED talk given by a monk named Andy Puddicombe at the TEDSalon London in fall 2012: blog.ted.com/2013/01/11/4 -scientific-studies-on-how-meditation-can-affect-your -heart-brain-and-creativity.

• Oliver Burkman's op-ed piece "The Power of Negative Thinking," *New York Times,* August 4, 2012, can be found here: www.nytimes .com/2012/08/05/opinion/sunday/the-positive-power-of-negative -thinking.html?_r = 0.

• Ohio State University psychology professor Richard Petty's three-part study on overcoming negative thinking is cited in "Bothered by Negative Thoughts? Just Throw Them Away" by Jeff Grabmeier in the Ohio State University *Research and Innovation Communication,* November 26, 2012; researchnews.osu.edu/archive/matthoughts.htm.

CHAPTER 3

• Amie M. Gordon's research on the role of gratitude in healthy romantic relationships can be found in a study by Amie M. Gordon, Emily A. Impett, Aleksandr Kogan, Christopher Oveis, and Dacher Keltner, "To Have and to Hold: Gratitude Promotes Relationship Maintenance in Intimate Bonds," *Journal of Personality and Social Psychology* 103, no. 2 (August 2012): 257–274. Gordon has written several articles on the subject as well, including these two: Amie M. Gordon, "Between You and Me: Why Some Relationships Work—and Others Don't," *Psychology Today,* March 1, 2013; www.psychologytoday.com/blog/between-you-and-me/201303/is-gratitude-the-antidote-relationship-failure; and Amie M. Gordon, "Gratitude Is for Lovers," *Greater Good,* February 5, 2013; greatergood.berkeley.edu/article/item/gratitude_is_for_lovers.

• How gratitude can get you through tough times: Jason Marsh, Lauren Klein, and Jeremy Adam Smith, "The Top 10 Insights from the 'Science of a Meaningful Life' in 2012," *Greater Good,* January 3, 2013; greatergood.berkeley.edu/article/item/the_top_insights_from_the_science_of_a_meaningful_life_in_2012.

• Dr. Terri Orbuch's thoughts on what makes the happiest couples can be found in "Improve Your Marriage with One Little Word," *Huffington Post,* November 22, 2011; www.huffingtonpost.com/dr-terri-orbuch/marriage-relationship-advice_b_1104814.html. Please also see her book, *5 Simple Steps to Take Your Marriage from Good to Great* (New York: Delacorte, 2009).

CHAPTER 5

• Dr. Marshall Duke and Dr. Robyn Fivush's Do You Know Scale: www.huffingtonpost.com/marshall-p-duke/the-stories-that-bind -us-_b_2918975.html.

• Bruce Feiler, "The Stories that Bind Us," *New York Times,* March 14, 2013; www.nytimes.com/2013/03/17/fashion/the-family-stories -that-bind-us-this-life.html?pagewanted = all&_r = 1&.

• Marshall P. Duke, "The Stories that Bind Us: What Are the Twenty Questions?" *Huffington Post,* March 23, 2013; www.huffingtonpost .com/marshall-p-duke/the-stories-that-bind-us-_b_2918975.html.

CHAPTER 6

• For a discussion on hope, please see psychology professor C. R. Snyder's "Approaching Hope" in *SGI Quarterly,* January 2006, which is drawn from his study published in the *Journal of Personality and Social Psychology* 60; www.sgiquarterly.org/feature2006Jan-2.html.

• How friends can make us healthy:
  — Tara Parker-Pope, "What Are Friends For? A Longer Life," *New York Times,* April 20, 2009; www.nytimes.com/2009/04/21 /health/21well.html?_r = 0.
  — Susan Gilbert, "Social Ties Reduce Risk of Cold," *New York Times,* June 25, 1997; www.nytimes.com/1997/06/25/us /social-ties-reduce-risk-of-a-cold.html?src = pm.

CHAPTER 7

• How we spend our time, at work and at home:
  — "OECD Reveals Countries with Longest Working Hours," *Huffington Post,* May 24, 2012; www.huffingtonpost.com /2012/05/24/11-countries-with-the-longest-working -hours_n_1543145.html.

— "How Much Time on Average Is Spent in the Bathroom Over a Lifetime?" Answer.com; wiki.answers.com/Q/How _much_time_on_average_is_spent_in_the_bathroom_over _a_lifetime.
— Lisa Belkin, "Time Wasted? Perhaps It's Well Spent," *New York Times,* May 31, 2007; www.nytimes.com/2007/05/31 /fashion/31work.html?_r = 0.

• Why people leave their jobs:

— Linda Oien, "People Quit Their Boss, Not Their Job: 4 Keys to Attracting and Retaining the Best and Brightest," business-PATHS, 2011; businesspaths.net/Articles/12/people-quit-their -boss-not-their-job.
— "No. 1 Reason People Quit Their Jobs" by the editors at Netscape; webcenters.netscape.compuserve.com/whats new/package.jsp?name = fte/quitjobs/quitjobs&floc = wn -dx.

• What motivates workers to do a good job:

— "APA Survey Finds Feeling Valued at Work Linked to Well-Being and Performance," American Psychological Association, March 8, 2012, announcing the APA's Stress in the Workplace Survey; www.apa.org/news/press/releases/2012 /03/well-being.aspx.
— On the Law of Effect, please see Clifford N. Lazarus, "Are You Teaching People to Treat You Badly?" *Psychology Today,* September 22, 2011; www.psychologytoday.com/blog/think -well/201109/are-you-teaching-people-treat-you-badly.

CHAPTER 8

• The benefits of generosity: Jason Marsh and Jill Suttie, "5 Ways Giving Is Good for You," *Greater Good,* December 13, 2010; greatergood .berkeley.edu/article/item/5_ways_giving_is_good_for_you.

• For the story of Julio Diaz or any of the other 40,000 stories collected by StoryCorps, please visit StoryCorps.org.

• For Giuliana Rancic's breast cancer journey, please see Diane Mapes's story about her on the *Today* show website, Today.com, including links to a video of Giuliana's announcement on *Today* about her illness and her decision to have a double mastectomy: www .today.com/id/45556523/site/todayshow/ns/today-today_health/t /giuliana-rancic-my-celebrity-breast-cancer-twin/#.UQFw_SovUXw.

CHAPTER 9

• The benefits of optimism:

— Emily Esfahani Smith, "The Benefits of Optimism Are Real," *The Atlantic,* March 1, 2013; www.theatlantic.com/ health/archive/2013/03/the-benefits-of-optimism-are-real /273306.

— Christopher Peterson, Martin Seligman, and G. E. Vaillant, "Pessimistic Explanatory Style Is a Risk Factor for Physical Illness: A Thirty-five-year Longitudinal Study," US National Library of Medicine and the National Institutes of Health, 1988.

— For further reading on Martin Seligman's work on optimism, check out his books, including *Authentic Happiness* (New York: Free Press, 2002), *Learned Optimism* (New York: Knopf, 1991), *What You Can Change & What You Can't* (New York: Knopf, 1993).

— Susan Biali, MD, "Don't Worry, Be Happy: The Surprising Benefits of Optimism," *Psychology Today,* November 11, 2009; www.psychologytoday.com/blog/prescriptions-life/200911 /dont-worry-be-happy-the-surprising-benefits-optimism.

— For more on J.R. Martinez's amazing story of personal triumph over adversity, see his book (with Alexandra Rockey Fleming), *Full of Heart: My Story of Survival, Strength, and Spirit* (New York: Hyperion, 2012).

— For more on Jim Harrison, see "'Man with the Golden Arm' Saves 2 Million Babies in Half a Century of Donating Rare Type of Blood," *Daily Mail,* March 22, 2010; www.dailymail.co.uk/news/article-1259627/Man-golden-arm-James-Harrison-saves-2million-babies-half-century-donating-rare-blood.html#ixzz2Ys8Es5r5.

CHAPTER 10

• The benefits of gratitude: "Gratitude Healthy: 10 Reasons Why Being Thankful Is Good for You," *Huffington Post,* November 22, 2012; www.huffingtonpost.com/2012/11/22/gratitude-healthy-benefits_n_2147182.html#slide = more263959.

• Twitter data comes from the Touch Agency: www.touchagency.com/touch-agency-twitter-infographic.

IN THE INTEREST OF PAYING IT FORWARD, I WANTED TO also include a section with information on some of my favorite sources and examples. Enjoy!

STATIONERY

www.NestingShoppe.com. I have been lucky enough to have their help in designing stationery for numerous occasions. Jessie Preza is always incredibly creative and wonderful to work with. If you need a matching thank-you note and return address label, no problem. She has everything you need when it comes to stationery. She also designed my website, and I couldn't love it more!!

www.Kidecals.com. Besides offering labels and stickers for home and school use, Kidecals can make custom return address labels out of your favorite photos. I have them for our entire family, as well as individual ones for Max, Blakesley, me and Ryan, and the two kids together—I love 'em that much!

www.StampedPaperCo.com. After working with Jill Efrussy on our 2010 Christmas card, as well as Blakesley's second and fourth birthday party invitations, I can't rave enough about what she creates. Her enthusiasm and joy for what she does truly shines through, even in the simplest of thank-you notes.

www.Minted.com. I was introduced to this community of designers by a friend who briefly worked for Minted in 2012 and have been an avid fan ever since—so much so that I used one of their designs to customize our 2012 Christmas card. I have their artwork on my walls and send personalized notes with their gorgeous stationery. I heart Minted!

www.GloryHaus.com. A dream of mine has always been to own a gift boutique—I'm obsessed with gifts! After receiving a Glory Haus picture frame from my friend Laura Lee, they became one of my favorite brands, and I could not be more thrilled to be partnering with them on a line of my own gifty goodies!! The Grateful Heart Collection by Glory Haus will include journals, picture frames, tote bags, wall art, jewelry, appreciation jars, and even pillows! To take a peek and place an order, please visit www.GloryHaus.com.

EXTRA-SPECIAL NOTES

Thanks to my type-A obsession with keeping a list of whom I write thank-you notes to, I calculated that I've handwritten at least six hundred over the past five years. (Now can you see why I have a bit of a paper fetish?)

With all that practice, I've definitely settled on a method: apologize in the event of a delay, keep it simple, reference the recipient's kindness and its effect, and speak from the heart.

Our family has also received very sweet notes of thanks over the years, and they give me constant inspiration for my next round of handwritten expressions of appreciation. Of course, it doesn't matter how simple the card is—what matters is that you take the time to express your gratitude. Extra-special notes can include an attached photo (one we received showed our friends' son wearing the T-shirt we gave him) or a handwritten message from your little one. No matter what you choose, a personal touch goes a long way.

YUMMY TREATS

We've either received tasty bites from these scrumptious eateries or worked with them to create delicious party treats and I would be remiss if I didn't share them with you all. If you order them as a gift or even for yourself, I promise you won't be disappointed.

www.GarrettPopcorn.com
www.JennyCookies.com
www.TooHauteCowgirls.com
www.VailGourmetCookieCo.com
www.Crumbs.com
www.StonewallKitchen.com

INSPIRATIONAL SITES

Always on the lookout for inspirational quotes or tweets or posts, I've compiled a few of my favorite sites. They are all on Twitter as well, if you want to get a regularly scheduled dose of goodness.

www.DailyGood.org
www.PositivelyPositive.com
www.GreaterGood.Berkeley.edu

And last but not least, please stay in touch with me at my recently launched website, www.TristaSutter.com, or on Twitter, @TristaSutter. As George Eliot said, "Blessed is the influence of one true loving human soul on another." I may not know you personally, but I feel blessed by our connection nonetheless. Thank you!

Acknowledgments

Everyone wants to be appreciated, so if you appreciate
someone, don't keep it a secret.

—MARY KAY ASH

IT IS NO SECRET THAT I FEEL FORTUNATE. I'VE SPOKEN about the many blessings of my life in the pages you've read, but I would be remiss if I didn't formally acknowledge them and (hopefully) everyone who made this book possible. Here goes (with crossed fingers that I don't forget anyone!) . . .

First and foremost—Ryan Sutter, I love you. I appreciate you. I thank you. Without your love, support, patience, understanding, constructively critical eye and ear, and incredible devotion to our beautiful babies, I couldn't have come close to completing this often overwhelming but exhilarating task. You gave me the space and time, but even more than that—you gave me the inspiration. You are, and always will be, my happily ever after.

To the tiny humans who take up the biggest space in my heart—Maxwell Alston and Blakesley Grace—thank you for allowing me the privilege of being your mama. You have taught me

Acknowledgments

more about living life with gratitude in your short years here on earth than I learned in the thirty-plus years before you made my dreams of being a mommy come true. Along with your daddy, you will always be my greatest treasure, the source of my truest joy, and the most favorite part of my day. I love you to the moon and back, to the moon and back, to the moon and back, to infinity and beyond!

To my always supportive, hug-loving momma—your brave willingness to allow me to tell your story of heartache and answered prayers made me love and appreciate you more than I ever have . . . and that's sayin' something. Thank you.

And same goes to you, Kathy. Your strength and openness are a true inspiration and I am proud to call you my sister.

To the in-laws that are anything but what that word usually conjures up, Barb and Bob Sutter, I owe you a *huge* debt of gratitude for graciously, frequently, and caringly loving on Mr. Max, Ms. B, and even Tankster. I honestly don't know that I could've finished my manuscript without your generosity of time and energy and will forever be grateful for your presence in my life and the lives of your grandbabies.

To my cherished friends who, without condition, took my babies under their protective and super-fun wings so that they could enjoy time with their best buddies while Mommy boringly sat in front of the computer, you are the best. This especially goes out to Kelly Holton and Kim Williams. My kids love your kids, but not as much as I love you.

To the Verlindes, thank you for regularly letting me escape up the stair tower for a peaceful spot (and one of the most gorgeous views in the Vail Valley) where I could soul-search, and get my creative juices flowing. And to Laura Lee, I absolutely *love* my grateful necklace! I had been hoping to do something similar in the jewelry world, but until my line is complete, your sweet gift gives me an almost daily reminder to take a page out of my own book.

To those who courageously faced the vulnerability of sharing their delicate life struggles (including Janet and John Herbert, J.R.,

Acknowledgments

the Bradfields, Jen, and Cookie) and those who allowed my readers a peek into their semi-private worlds through their well-written blogs, stories, and speeches (including Aunt Nancy, Catt, Jenny, Nipun, and K.L.)—I sincerely thank you. The fact that you trusted me to handle them with care is an honor that I'll never forget.

I believe that God has a plan for us all, but to those who have played an integral role in my life and helped guide me to the joy I know now—you will eternally be appreciated. That includes my immediate and extended family; the friends I've always considered family; Oprah Winfrey for her inspiration; Mike Fleiss, Lisa Levenson, and the Telepictures/Warner Horizon/ABC team for the once-in-a-lifetime chance at love; the rest of my Bachelor family; and the heavens above for both answered and unanswered prayers.

To all the parents who had their kids play along with the "What are you grateful for?" game . . .

To the sitters who kept my active kiddos company while I feverishly tried to meet deadlines . . .

To anyone who offered up their assistance for content that I just couldn't seem to wrangle on my own (including Missy, Evin, Erik, Stephanie, Allie, Nathalie, Bernard, Tracey, Casley, Amy, DeWayne, Jen, and Ellen) . . .

To Michael Lavine, ShopItToMe.com, Katelyn Simkins, and the rest of the cover crew for helping me put my best face forward and dealing with a day of kiddo chaos . . .

To anyone and everyone who sent much-needed and appreciated words of encouragement through social media when I had hit the wall of writer's block . . .

To all those who responded to my Facebook and Twitter requests for tips, information, and inspiration that I could use to spread the word of gratitude . . .

Thank you. *Thank you.* Thank You. THANK YOU. *THANK YOU.* **THANK YOU!!!!!!!!!**

And last but *certainly* not least, to all those who have led me to the literary path I so thankfully began traveling on three years ago, consider yourself virtually hugged!

Acknowledgments

Babette . . . thank you for introducing me to Celeste!

Celeste . . . thank you for helping bring out my authentic voice, providing unequaled guidance, and always lifting me up when I needed a boost.

Sandra . . . thank you for helping me organize the initial chaos of my novice writer's brain into the sixty pages that would lead me to Da Capo.

Liz . . . thank you for your creative input, gracious wisdom, and acceptance of *way* too many smiley faces. ☺

And to everyone at Da Capo Press and the Perseus Books Group: Thank you for welcoming me into your enchanting family and changing my life. From all those who gave me the special opportunity to break bread, shake their hand, and personally tell them the story of my stories; to Jonathan, who had to continuously put up with my overly critical eye for detail; to Kevin and Lissa for kindly working with me to come up with a picture-perfect plan of attack; to John, Lindsey, Carolyn, and Antoinette.

And finally, to my *wonderful* editor, Renee, thank you for believing in me and my idea, gently nudging me in a writer's direction, helping mold my words into just the right content and rhythm, and thoughtfully understanding my struggles. Your unfaltering encouragement was the key in helping me spread my wings to fly toward the title of "author." Ever so humbly, thank you.

As Thomas Wilder once said, "We can only be said to be alive in those moments when our hearts are conscious of our treasures." I say with certainty that I am not only living, but I am alive.